# Addressing the Human Capital Crisis in the Federal Government:

## A Knowledge Management Perspective

# Addressing the Human Capital Crisis in the Federal Government:

## A Knowledge Management Perspective

DR. JAY LIEBOWITZ

BUTTERWORTH HEINEMANN

**An imprint of Elsevier**

Amsterdam, Boston, Heidelberg, London, New York, Oxford, Paris,
San Diego, San Francisco, Singapore, Sydney, Tokyo

Butterworth–Heinemann is an imprint of Elsevier.



∞ Recognizing the importance of preserving what has been written, Elsevier prints its books on acid-free paper whenever possible.

**Library of Congress Cataloging-in-Publication Data**

Liebowitz, Jay, 1957–
Addressing the human capital crisis in the Federal Government : a knowledge management perspective / Jay Liebowitz.
p. cm.
Includes bibliographical references and index.
ISBN 0-7506-7713-9
1. Civil service—United States—Personnel management. 2. Human capital—United States. 3. Knowledge management–United States. I. Title.

JK765.L54 2004
352.6′0973—dc21 2003052357

**British Library Cataloguing-in-Publication Data**
A catalogue record for this book is available from the British Library.

The publisher offers special discounts on bulk orders of this book. For information, please contact:

Manager of Special Sales
Elsevier
200 Wheeler Road
Burlington, MA 01803
Tel: 781-313-4700
Fax: 781-313-4882

For information on all Butterworth–Heinemann publications available, contact our World Wide Web home page at: http://www.bh.com

10 9 8 7 6 5 4 3 2 1

Printed in the United States of America

To the younger generations—the future "human capital,"

and

To the seven NASA astronauts on STS-107 whose memories will live forever!

# Contents

**Preface** xi

1. A Broad View of Human Capital 1

Is Human Resources the Same as Human Capital? 5
What Should Be the Attributes of a Chief Human Capital Officer? 10
Linking Human Capital to Knowledge Management 11

2. The Human Capital Crisis in the Federal Government 15

Statistics Abound . . . 15
How Did We Get into This Mess? 17
A Case in Point 19
Industry Is Also Experiencing Similar Human Capital Challenges 23
Are Other Governments Experiencing Similar Human Capital Crises? 25
So, What Is Being Done about It? 26

3. Developing a Human Capital Strategy 31

What Human Capital Strategy Models and Measures Are Available in the Federal Government? 33
An Agency Developing Its Human Capital Strategy: The Internal Revenue Service 40
Developing an Approach for Constructing a Human Capital Strategy 42

4. The Four Pillars of Human Capital 45

The Essentials of a Human Capital Strategy 48
To Summarize . . . 59

5. Knowledge Management: The Key Pillar in a Human Capital Strategy 61

Knowledge Management 63
Lessons Learned from the Trenches 64
Crafting a Knowledge Management Strategy 67
Implementing a Knowledge Management Strategy as Part of a Human Capital Strategy 73

6. Pillar Two: Performance Management through a Knowledge Management Lens 77

Enhancing Performance Management through Knowledge Management 80
How Knowledge Management May Improve Performance Management 87

7. Competency Management: A Necessary Pillar in a Human Capital Strategy 93

Knowledge Management and Competency Management 99

8. Change Management: The Forgotten Pillar 105

Change Management in Knowledge Management and Vice Versa 107
NASA: Applying Change Management Strategies 111
Integrated Financial Management Program Change Management 112
Change Management, Knowledge Management, and Human Capital 114

9. Establishing Strategic Partnerships for Human Capital 117

Using Online Communities to Strengthen Human Capital 124
Linking with Universities for Stimulating an Organization's Intellectual Capital 125
What's Ahead? 126

10. Strategic Management of Human Capital: The Future 127

The Need to Further Leverage Informal Networks in Organizations 128
Tapping into the Senior Workforce 129
Building the "Organizational Intelligence" 133
Knowledge Management Technology 134
Recommendation for Reform 135
Final Thoughts 137

Case Study: An Operational Study of Knowledge Management Activities at the ABC Foundation 139

Introduction 139
Knowledge Management Implementation Critical Success Factors 142
Knowledge Management–Related Initiatives at ABC Foundation 145
Discussion 148
Summary 165
References 165

GAO Report: Human Capital: Practices That Empowered and Involved Employees 169

**Index** 213

# Preface

The number one government-wide initiative, as outlined in President Bush's "President's Management Agenda," is the strategic management of human capital. According to Knowledgeworkers.com, human capital is the accumulated value of an individual's intellect, knowledge, and experience. In the U.S. federal government, a human capital crisis exists. The factors contributing to a human capital dilemma include a knowledge bleed due to retirement eligibility, changing perspectives on work, and escalating knowledge loss. According to a Joint Hearing on the Federal Human Capital, by 2005 more than half of the 1.8 million non-postal civilian employees will be eligible for early or regular retirement. An even greater percentage of the Senior Executive Service, the government's core managers, will be eligible to leave.

All government agencies are now wrestling with how best to develop a human capital strategy for their organization. Many of these agencies have scored a "red" (lowest rating) on the Government Scorecard in the way they are approaching their strategic management of human capital.

This book takes a collective look at the existing human capital frameworks being used in government and provides a unifying structure, with four key pillars, on which government agencies can develop their human capital strategy. Using a knowledge management perspective on which to base the insights important to developing a human capital strategy, this book provides extremely timely and informative help to the government agencies addressing a human capital crisis. I hope that it will be a key reference for government agencies to follow in developing their human capital strategy. It is geared primarily for federal senior executives, human capital planners and managers, knowledge managers, and organizational development professionals in government as well as in industry and academe.

I would like to thank Karen Maloney, Katie Hennessy, Dennis McGonagle, Mamata Reddy, and the rest of the staff at Elsevier for publishing this book. I would also like to thank my colleagues in government, industry, and academia for helping me to shape and refine my views, especially Shereen Remez, Lee Salmon, and Alex Bennet for their encouragement *and* endorsements. The views expressed are my own, and not the official views of the organizations mentioned.

I also want to thank my colleagues and students at Johns Hopkins University for encouraging me to write this book. And most of all, my family deserves my adoration for allowing me to sneak upstairs to complete this book. Enjoy!

Jay Liebowitz
Johns Hopkins University
jliebow1@jhu.edu

# ONE

# A Broad View of Human Capital

Senior executives have been claiming for years that people are the organization's greatest asset. Chief executive officers typically state that their employees give the company its most competitive edge. Some people, on the other hand, state that individuals are replaceable, but is that really the case? Think about the situation where your leading expert will be retiring shortly and what you will do to replace his or her experience and expertise when this expert leaves. Or ponder how best the organization can leverage and share the knowledge of its employees and customers in order to stimulate innovation, promote a greater sense of belonging and community, and improve decision-making.

Organizations are rapidly realizing that their employees' *brainpower* is what distinguishes them from their competitors—and it's not the one or two shining stars in the organization; it's the collective synergy of the organization's employee workforce. There have been baseball teams that have made it to the World Series without having many named players. It's the knowledge sharing process and the ability to work well with each other that has contributed to the success of many ball clubs. The same is true of organizations. The collective talent of the employees (including management) can provide a powerful mechanism for ensuring organizational success. Their collective wisdom can be transformed into organizational intelligence whereby the organization can become an agile, adaptive learning organization. The key to making this happen comes back to "the people" or the organization's "human capital."

What do we mean by "human capital"? Brainmarket Corporation defines human capital as a loose catchall term for the practical knowledge, acquired skills, and learned abilities of an individual that make him or her potentially productive and thus equip him or her to earn income in exchange for labor. Josefek (University of Southern California) and Kauffman (University of Minnesota) define human capital as the stock of knowledge, skills, and abilities embedded in an individual that results from natural endowment and subsequent investment in education, training, and experience. NASA Goddard Space Flight Center refers to human capital as the entire talent pool (including civil servants, contractors, NASA HQ, NASA Centers, international partners, and universities) that contributes to Goddard's mission.

We define "human capital" as the collective experience, knowledge, and expertise of those contributing to an organization's mission. We are primarily interested in the organization's employees and the knowledge they hold, but we also take a broader view that human capital includes other constituencies that are central to the organization's mission (e.g., contractors, customers, international partners, universities, etc.). The focus, however, is on the organization's employees (or the Federal civil servants if referring to the U.S. government) and the brainpower they possess. Once their role is further identified, then supporting roles can be provided by the other important human capital groups.

The working human capital definition above is consistent with the knowledge management community's sense of human capital. In the knowledge management world, intellectual capital is the sum of human capital, structural capital, and customer capital. Human capital refers to the "brainpower" of the employees. Structural capital refers to what one can't easily take home from the office (e.g., intellectual property rights, certain databases, etc.). Customer capital, sometimes called social or relationship capital, is the knowledge learned from the organization's customers. In fact, according to the "State of Knowledge Management in 2001 Survey," as discussed in the May 2001 issue of *Knowledge Management Magazine*, the number one reason by far for adopting knowledge management is to retain the expertise of personnel (51.9 percent)—a human capital reason. Additionally, the same survey indicated that the top business use of knowledge management initiatives (77.7 percent) is to capture and share best practices. Again, the knowledge capture and sharing activities among the individuals in the organization indicate a human capital theme.

Why are organizations, especially the U.S. Government, concerned about their human capital situation? Why is the strategic management of human capital important enough to list as the top government-wide initiative as outlined in President Bush's "President's Management Agenda"? And why are most U.S. government agencies getting a "red" score in their strategic management of human capital efforts?

Let's take a look at some numbers. In the U.S. Government, about 53 percent of the federal civil servants are eligible to retire in the next five years. About 71 percent of these individuals are the senior executives in the U.S. Government. As an example, at NASA Goddard, about 28 percent of the 3,200 federal civil servants are eligible to retire in the next five years, with the current average age being 46. About 45 percent of the scientists at NASA Goddard (53 being the average current age) are eligible to retire in the next five years. Additionally, at NASA Goddard a preliminary survey indicated that about 112 areas were identified as potential "at risk" knowledge gaps whereby the expert would be retiring in one to three years with no backup expert to fill in. Out of these 112 areas, 64 were cited as being strategic to Goddard's mission. NASA Goddard, NASA as an agency, and most of the other U.S. Government agencies are experiencing similar (and more severe) human capital pangs.

Besides NASA, other government agencies are witnessing human capital shortage problems. According to the Health Physics Society, a critical shortage exists in the supply of qualified radiation safety professionals throughout a broad spectrum of activities within the United States, including medical practice and research, regulatory oversight, academic research, environmental protection, occupational safety, and the research and application of nuclear technologies. The July 2002 *Corporate Training Monthly* publication indicates that Canada, and Alberta in particular, is facing a human capital crisis—a shortage of highly skilled workers who are necessary to ensuring the country's growth and prosperity through the next decade and beyond.

The ensuing human capital crisis is not only in the U.S. Government; businesses and not-for-profit organizations are experiencing similar woes. For example, in September 2002, leading U.S. business executives met for the First Talent 10 Symposium to discuss the impact of the forecasted labor shortage. The U.S. Bureau of Labor Statistics indicated that the national shortage of workers in all occupations will reach the 35,000 mark by 2010. The impact of the labor shortage will be felt shortly in the transportation and agriculture industries.

According to Bill Sebra, CEO of Knowledge Workers, Inc., many factors have contributed to the growing importance of human capital management. With the shortage of qualified technology workers increasing as the "baby boom" generation retires and technology worker turnover rates average 20 percent or higher, companies must plan today for the people that will lead their businesses tomorrow. Giga Group reports that the total cost of replacing a technology worker can be as high as 2.5 times the salary of the departing employee. A Merrill Lynch study on human capital management noted that the average person entering the work force today will work for between eight and ten different employers versus four to six just two decades ago.

In order to help retain and attract employees, knowledge management should be a key pillar forming the foundation of an organization's human capital strategy. Some of the early corporate adopters of knowledge management include Chevron, Cap Gemini Ernst & Young, and Schlumberger, and they have realized the importance of knowledge management for improving collaboration, knowledge retention and sharing, and a sense of belonging for employee recruiting and retention. The American Productivity and Quality Center shows that these organizations used online communities of practice to share knowledge among their employees and customers. As a result, Chevron produced a $2 billion reduction in annual operating costs. Cap Gemini Ernst & Young produced a ten-fold growth in revenue with a five-fold increase in employees. Schlumberger, by using technical communities of practice by putting knowledge in the hands of employees and customers, generated a $75 million first-year savings and a projected $100 million customer savings.

## Is Human Resources the Same as Human Capital?

Some organizations have traditionally thought of human resources as being the same as human capital. The functions that a human resources director (HRD) performs are usually not the same as envisioned by the emerging position called a Chief Human Capital Officer (or Chief People Officer). Granted there should be a close alliance with the HRD and the Chief Human Capital Officer, but the latter is more involved with a strategic view of the organization versus an operational perspective, as typically performed in the HR department. The HRD usually oversees such areas as personnel actions, career counseling, compensation and benefits, and employee performance and development. The Chief Human Capital Officer would develop workforce development strategies and align them with organization missions. As Bill Sebra of Knowledge Workers Inc. indicates, the time is ripe to have a Chief Human Capital Officer as over 70 percent of Fortune 1000 CEOs view human capital management as a strategic component of their business.

Legislation for U.S. government agencies to have a Chief Human Capital Officer has already been proposed. The legislation would create a Chief Human Capital Officer in each federal agency to do the following:

- Set the workforce development strategy of the agency;
- Assess current workforce characteristics and future needs based on the agency's strategic plan and mission;

- Align human resources policies with organization mission, strategic goals, and performance outcomes;
- Develop a culture of continuous learning to attract and retain high-performing employees;
- Identify best practices and benchmarking studies;
- Create systems for measuring intellectual capital and identifying links of that capital to organizational performance and growth.

Industry has already begun to appoint Chief Human Capital Officers. For example, Steven J. Becker is Senior Vice President and Chief Human Capital Officer of Fujitsu Transaction Solutions Inc. Becker, who joined Fujitsu in March 2002, oversees the company's human capital initiatives and is responsible for human resources, organizational development, corporate communications, knowledge management, and facilities management.

According to Susannah Figura's article "Human Capital: The Missing Link" in *Government Executive Magazine,* most federal managers and human resources specialists are still more focused on short-term needs than long-term ones. It would be better for human resources departments to be rated on a more strategic scale rather than a tactical one. Such rating criteria might be: conducts strategic analysis of present and future human resources needs and workforce planning; able to obtain needed employees; able to maintain a workforce with a mix of skills that matches its needs; and ability to motivate and reward employees to support strategic and performance goals. In fact, the Human Capital Scorecard, as advocated by the Office of Personnel Management's (OPM's) Human Resources Management Council, has five key dimensions: Strategic Alignment, Strategic Competencies, Leadership, Performance Culture, and Learning. These dimensions are derived from the September 1999 General Accounting Office Human Capital Report, which indicated five parts of a human capital framework:

1. *Strategic Planning:* establish the agency's mission, vision for the future, core values, goals, and strategies
2. *Organizational Alignment:* integrate human capital strategies with the agency's core business practices
3. *Leadership:* foster a committed leadership team and provide continuity through succession planning
4. *Talent:* recruit, hire, develop, and retain employees with the skills for mission accomplishment
5. *Performance Culture:* enable and motivate performance while ensuring accountability and fairness for all employees

In the Human Capital Scorecard and the GAO's human capital framework, the mapping of the dimensions is very similar. However, the learning dimension, as cited under the Human Capital Scorecard, is something that isn't covered explicitly in the GAO human capital framework. The learning dimension looks at how an organization can become an adaptive, agile, learning organization whereby a knowledge sharing culture is built and nurtured. Here, the theme of knowledge management is expressed and fits nicely within a "learning pillar."

According to the GAO Human Capital report, human capital has two key principles. First, people are assets whose value can be enhanced through investment. Skandia typically compares their organization to a tree. With a tree, there are hidden and visible components—the hidden ones are the roots and the visible ones are the blossoms and fruit. In order to get the tree to grow, you need to nourish the roots. In the same manner, the people and their intellectual capital in an organization are the roots, and to maximize their intellectual capital they must also be nourished in terms of training and development, mentoring, recognition and rewards, and so on. Second, an organization's human capital policies must be aligned to support the organization's shared vision.

In the GAO study, eight key concepts were common to the "best practiced" organizations:

1. Value people as assets rather than as costs.
2. Emphasize mission, vision, and organizational culture.
3. Hold managers responsible for achieving results instead of imposing rigid, process-oriented rules and standards.
4. Choose an organizational structure appropriate to the organization rather than trying to make "one size fit all."
5. Instead of isolating the "personnel function" organizationally, integrate human resource management into the mission of the organization.
6. Treat continuous learning as an investment in success rather than as a cost to be minimized.
7. Pursue an integrated rather than an ad hoc approach to information management.
8. Provide sustained leadership that recognizes change as a permanent condition, not a one-time event.

The GAO and OPM further stress the need for cultural transformation as a new model for government organizations. They indicate that government organizations will need to become less hierarchical, process-oriented, "stovepiped," and inwardly focused. They will need to become more partnerial, results-oriented, integrated, and externally focused. Government organizations will need to achieve better balance between results, client/customer, and employee issues, and that they will need to work better with other governmental organizations, nongovernmental organizations, and the private sector, both domestically and internationally, to achieve results. In fact, Victor Rezendes, the Managing Director of Strategic Issues for the U.S. General Accounting Office, feels that strategic human capital management is greatly needed whereby human capital is established as a top priority, a modern and high-performance–oriented human capital system is created, and updated human capital policies, procedures, and information systems are developed and implemented (http://www.gao.gov/cghome/hvd/sld030.htm). Rezendes believes that a three-phased approach for strategic human capital management is required: do everything administratively possible; seek incremental legislative changes when necessary and base them on a sound business case; and begin to build a consensus for comprehensive civil service reform based on an analysis of existing workforce challenges and selected demonstration projects.

It is becoming clear that to make strategic human capital management really happen in organizations, especially the government, a new position of Chief Human Capital Officer should be created. This is the direction that the U.S. government and industry seem to be taking. Some of the U.S. government agencies have Chief Human Resources Officers, as at the Internal Revenue Service. It is analogous to how Chief Information Officers, Chief Knowledge Officers (CKO), and Chief Learning Officers (CLO) have been created throughout business and government in recent years. There potentially could be some overlap between some of the roles and duties of a Chief Human Capital Officer and those of either a Chief Knowledge or Chief Learning Officer. Even though the Chief Human Capital Officer would probably have a broader charter than either the CKO or CLO, there are some similarities in terms of knowledge retention activities, building and nurturing a knowledge sharing culture, and transforming individualized learning into organizational learning. In the U.S. Government, there are a few CKO positions (as at the General Services Administration, or GSA, the U.S. Coast Guard, the U.S. Navy, etc.), but perhaps the creation of a Chief Human Capital Officer may subsume some of these duties. In industry, however, the CKO position is more prevalent than the equivalent position in the government. Thus, it will be interesting to see the interplay between the Chief Human Capital Officer and the Chief Knowledge Officer in industry.

## What Should Be the Attributes of a Chief Human Capital Officer?

As the Chief Human Capital Officer (CHCO) position emerges in both government and industry, what should be the essential attributes of such an individual? To help us answer this question, we can look at the attributes of Chief Knowledge Officers that compare favorably to the characteristics that a CHCO should possess. Robert Neilson, who works on the role of a CKO at the National Defense University, believes that the competencies that make a successful CKO are: communications (storyteller, avid communicator); strategic thinking; tools and techniques; personal behavior; personal knowledge and cognitive capability; leadership and management. Specifically, Neilson identifies the following necessary personal attributes for a CKO: passion, patience, persistence, sensitivity, organizational savvy, smart, wise, lifelong learner, thick-skinned, integrator, and depth and breadth of knowledge.

A Chief Human Capital Officer should also possess many of the same traits as the CKO; however, some of the major responsibilities would include: aligning human capital management and services with the strategic plan; monitoring human capital performance; advising the CEO/Secretary on human capital issues; consulting with and advising senior officers; reviewing human capital data analyses. A Chief Human Capital Officer exists for the new U.S. Department of Homeland Security. The CHCO would be responsible for developing and implementing reliable measures for self-assessment and improvement. The CHCO would be the focal point for the execution of workforce planning and development: attracting and retaining key talent; developing world-class leaders, managers, and supervisors; and creating a work environment where employees are empowered and challenged to perform their best.

How would the role of a CHCO differ from that of a Human Resources Director? One of the major differences is the strategic perspective and long-term view that the CHCO would have over the more operational view of a Human Resources Director. Linking the organization's strategic goals to its human capital investments and developing a "learning" organization are two primary responsibilities that the CHCO would have that may distinguish this position from that of a Human Resources Director. Establishing a workforce development strategy for the organization is an important activity that the CHCO would undertake.

## Linking Human Capital to Knowledge Management

Knowledge management is the process of creating value from an organization's intangible assets. Simply put, knowledge management deals with how best to leverage knowledge internally and externally. Knowledge management is concerned with how to capture, share, apply, and create knowledge throughout the organization and for the organization's stakeholders. The knowledge comes from the organization's employees, customers, stakeholders, retirees, contractors, partners, and other knowledge sources. This knowledge base is derived from the organization's human capital.

The human capital in an organization primarily emanates from the "brainpower" of the organization's employees. The sharing of lessons learned, best practices, cases, stories, and anecdotes are examples of how knowledge can be passed from one individual to another. Mentoring is a wonderful way to share the tacit knowledge of an expert with the mentee. Finding ways to preserve, share, replenish, and grow knowledge are important objectives for a knowledge management, and human capital, strategy. Identifying the core competencies of the organization and understanding the organization's mission, strategy, and business goals are critical elements that need to be determined before a knowledge management or human capital strategy can be developed. The knowledge management and human capital strategy should be aligned with the organizational mission and strategy in order to maximize the contributions of the organization's human capital.

At NASA Goddard Space Flight Center (GSFC), the Knowledge Management Officer created a mapping of the knowledge management (KM) strategy based upon the overall strategy and goals of the organization, as shown in Figure 1.1. The Knowledge Management Officer at NASA Goddard learned some valuable lessons to help organizations use knowledge management effectively and counteract the criticism sometimes associated with knowledge management. First, it is easier to apply knowledge management strategies that fit an organization's culture than to first change the organizational culture and then apply knowledge management. For a large organization, academic studies indicate that it takes ten to fourteen years to change an organization's culture. In order to show some quick wins from KM to

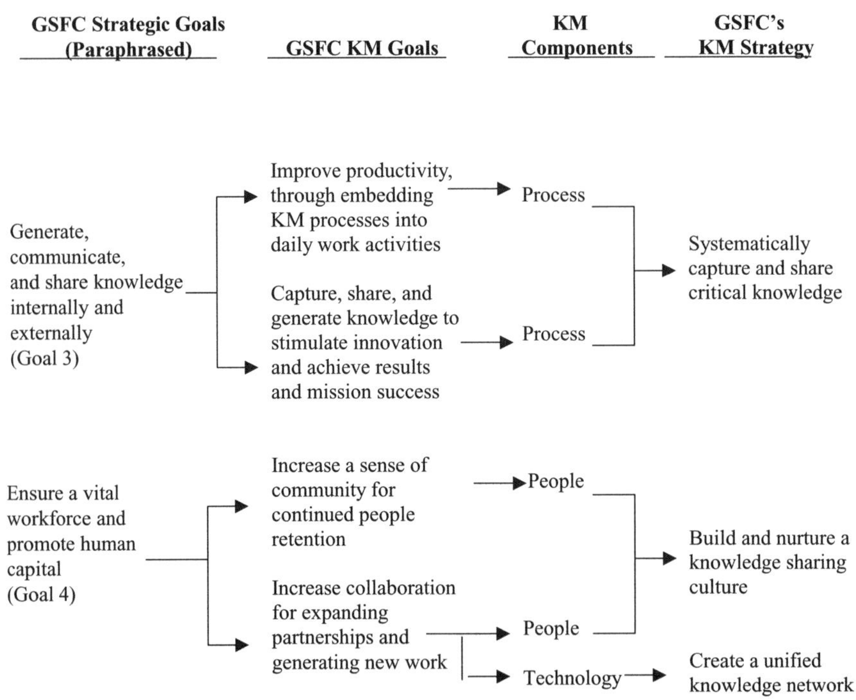


FIGURE 1.1 *Linking Knowledge Management to Organizational Strategies at NASA Goddard Space Flight Center (GSFC).*

overcome skepticism, we don't have the luxury of time to wait for the organization's culture to change before applying KM. Use knowledge management strategically by aligning it with the particular subculture where it will be used. This will eliminate some of the resistance to change and allow KM to have a greater likelihood of success.

Second, don't try to do everything at once. Develop a knowledge management strategic plan for the organization, and then have a two to three year knowledge management implementation plan to carry out the strategy. For example, at NASA Goddard, a two-year knowledge management implementation plan was developed whereby the first year was devoted to creating an awareness of KM at all levels of the organization, educating people on KM, initiating quick-win KM pilots with metrics for success (peppered throughout the organization), developing the technology infrastructure to support knowledge sharing, and incorporating KM into the organization's human capital strategy. The second year was devoted to developing the organizational infrastructure to support knowledge management, embedding KM processes into the daily working activities of the employees, developing a recognition and reward system to promote knowledge sharing behaviors, and expanding the KM pilots into full-fledged KM projects.

Third, apply knowledge management to the core competencies of the organization and show value-added benefits. At Goddard, for example, developing satellite missions and projects is one of the core areas. By injecting knowledge management into these satellite projects, stories can then be told about how knowledge management helped to improve productivity or increase collaboration to achieve results and mission success. If another project hears this story, then this project and others will most likely want to apply KM as well in order to better address their mission goals.

Fourth, there will always be skeptics of anything. With knowledge management, the same holds true. Some people may feel that it is the "management fad of the day." Others will see the real value that knowledge management may bring to the organization. Link up with the KM advocates early on to build a cadre of KM spokespersons. This could be through a KM working group (comprised of advocates from across the organization, as we had done at Goddard) and through having the support of senior leadership (who typically seem to appreciate the value of knowledge management and human capital in an organization). It is also important to use both a bottom-up and top-down strategy in gaining support for KM. By exciting the working levels of the organization on the virtues of KM, they will tell their management who will in turn tell their leadership. A top-down approach is also helpful, as the organization sees that there is senior sponsorship and support for KM activities.

Last, don't put the cart before the horse. Try not to force-fit solutions to requirements. In other words, try to find out the "pains" of the organization in terms of business needs and then see how knowledge management might be able to address these pains.

Whether you want to call "knowledge management" by that name or some other alias such as "knowledge sharing," "working better together," "leveraging knowledge," or the like, it is up to you to assess what works best for your organization. The bottom line is that KM should be a key pillar in an organization's human capital strategy. Without it, organizations will be missing the mark in the near future!

# TWO
# The Human Capital Crisis in the Federal Government

## Statistics Abound . . .

U.S. Senator George Voinovich from Ohio warned of the U.S. federal human capital crisis in 2000 in the "Report to the President: The Crisis in Human Capital," prepared by the Subcommittee on Oversight of Government Management, Restructuring, and the District of Columbia. At that time, Senator Voinovich indicated that more than half of the federal workforce would be eligible to leave (retire) in just four years. Part of the problem causing this ensuing crisis was due to poor planning during the government's downsizing in the 1990s, the agencies' inabilities to compete with the private sector for talented workers, and insufficient commitment to training and development. According to Jason Peckenpaugh's *Government Executive* article "Report Outlines Ways to Improve the Federal Workforce" on December 5, 2000, the NASA Inspector General testified that she constantly loses qualified candidates to the private sector because it takes an average of four to six months for candidates to navigate the federal hiring process. The report identified some ways to reform and rejuvenate the federal workforce including: agencies having limited "direct" or "on-the-spot" hiring authority for information technology positions and outstanding applicants; training budgets should be centralized and given their own line item in agency budgets; and agencies should have greater flexibility to experiment with broad-banding payment systems (http://207.27.3.29/dailyfed/1200/120500p1.htm).

In July 2001, David Walker (the Comptroller General of the United States at the General Accounting Office) indicated that the key competitive element in the twenty-first century is people. He noted that the human capital crisis extends to the "IT" (information technology) workforce in the federal government. Walker pointed out that the U.S. Bureau of Labor Statistics projects that demand for computer systems analysts, engineers, and scientists will almost double between 1998 and 2008, and that the demand for computer programmers will increase by 30 percent during this same time period. For the federal computer specialist series, Walker and the GAO estimated that 30 percent of these employees would be eligible to retire by the end of FY2006 and that 14 percent would actually retire by then. The numbers are even higher for telecommunications and program management series. State and local governments, as well as the private sector, also face similar IT human capital challenges (http://www.gao.gov/cghome/ia/egov.htm).

According to U.S. Government figures, 53 percent of the federal civil servants are eligible to retire in the next five years, and 71 percent of those are in the Senior Executive Service (SES) (http://www.fedmanagers.org/help_ease_human_capital_crisis_fehbp.htm). The Office of Personnel Management (OPM) wants agencies to go from 180 to 30 days for hiring and to accelerate the SES selection process. In some agencies, such as NASA, there are at least twice as many people in the over-60 age group in certain job classifications as those in the under-30 age group. A January 21, 2002, *Government Computer News* article by Preeti Vasishtha indicates that a poll commissioned by the Council for Excellence in Government after the September 11, 2001, terrorist attacks tragic event showed that although people between 18 and 29 years old look more favorably on government jobs than do older workers, more than 80 percent of college-educated Americans reject Uncle Sam as a potential employer. According to Pamela Ferdinand's *Washington Post* article "But Do You Want Uncle

Sam?" (November 21, 2001), the federal government has reduced its workforce by 20 percent since 1993, and some projects indicate that the government faces a further dramatic shedding of baby boomer employees eligible for retirement over the next five years. Various Congresspersons, such as former Representative Constance Morella and others, feel that "human capital" experts should be part of any public agency's executive team and that management cadres should be fostered government-wide. A basic problem has been that the federal government has failed to adequately recruit, retain, and train workers for the twenty-first century.

## How Did We Get into This Mess?

In Matthew Weinstock's *Government Executive Magazine* article "Human Capital" (May 1, 2001), the GAO cited some examples of our federal human capital crisis:

- *NASA:* The loss of staff and critical skill sets poses potentially serious problems for the safety and planned flight rate of future space shuttle missions.
- *Nuclear Regulatory Commission:* The agency's inability to retain people with skills necessary to "achieve its mission and fill the gaps created by growing retirement eligibilities could be threatened by the decline in university enrollments in nuclear engineering and other fields related to nuclear safety."
- *Social Security Administration:* Increasing demand for services, the imminent retirement of a large part of its workforce, changing customer expectations, and mixed results of utilizing new technology will challenge the agency's ability to distribute benefits more quickly and accurately.
- *Agency for International Development:* Staffing shortfalls in the procurement area hamper the agency's ability to initiate and monitor contracts.

There are many factors that contribute to the ensuing human capital crisis in the U.S. government. One key factor is that we have been downsizing the federal civilian workforce over the past decade. In David Walker's talk at the E-Gov 2001 conference, he indicated that our federal workforce has been shrinking consistently over the past decade (from 2.3 million federal civil servants in 1990 to 1.9 million in 2000). Essentially, the U.S. federal workforce has been trying to do more with less. In the 1990s the federal government cut back on hiring new people; now, many organizations, like NASA, are feeling the effects. The GAO in its "Report to the President: The Crisis in Human Capital" cited these findings:

- The National Aeronautics and Space Administration (NASA) found that personnel cuts involving the elimination of one-third of the space shuttle's program staff affected the agency's ability to support shuttle flights safely.
- The U.S. Forest Service's ability to respond to catastrophic fires has been limited by recent losses in experienced firefighters and foresters, among other staff. Shortages of workers required to direct operations and fight the massive public land fires in the summer of 2000 revealed this vulnerability.
- The Department of Defense lost nearly 400,000 civilian employees (about 36 percent) during the 1990s, leading to growing concern about the Pentagon's ability to achieve its future weapons acquisition and logistics objectives.
- The Department of Energy faces growing management instability as a result of downsizing and retirements. Its Stockpile Stewardship Program, responsible for maintaining the nation's existing nuclear warhead and component stock, has seen a dramatic increase in the number of offices that are vacant or operating with acting managers (from 17 percent in 1996 to about 65 percent in 2000).
- More than 80 percent of senior managers at the Department of Veterans Affairs will be eligible for retirement by 2005.

- Certain agencies with historically low levels of SES retirements (e.g., the Environmental Protection Agency) are expected to see retirement rates more than double by 2005.
- As many as 90 percent of senior-level criminal investigators are eligible for retirement by 2005, creating the potential for havoc at agencies such as the Federal Bureau of Investigation, Customs Service, Drug Enforcement Administration, and Secret Service.
- The Department of Defense could lose up to half of its civilian acquisition workforce, as more than 50 percent of these employees are eligible to retire by 2005 as well.

Many of these examples are the result of government downsizing over the past decade, the "graying" workforce, little infusion of new, young talent into the government, the mobility and changing work patterns of entering workers, lack of interest in working for the federal government due to salary shortfalls in the government versus those in the private sector, lack of adequate mentoring and workforce planning, and many other reasons.

## A Case in Point

The federal civilian workforce at the National Aeronautics and Space Administration (NASA) has been generally shrinking over the years, as shown in the chart in Figure 2.1, from the NASA Office of Human Resources website.

The Senior Executive Service (SES) workforce at NASA has also generally decreased over the years, and the average age of an SES individual has been increasing across the various NASA Centers, as shown in Figures 2.2 and 2.3.

In looking towards the future, NASA's civilian workforce will still be getting smaller. According to NASA's Office of Human Resources, "seven out of ten NASA Centers have reached their target employment levels and can now revitalize their staff as new losses occur. Three

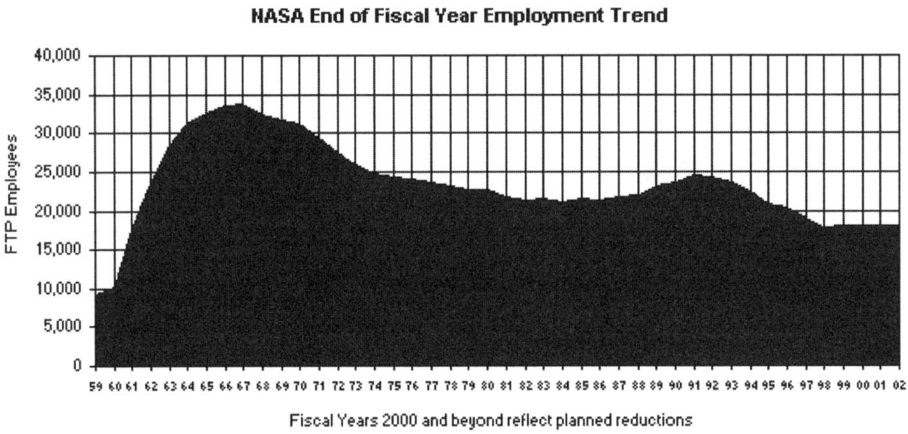


FIGURE 2.1 *NASA End of Fiscal Year Employment Trend (Source: http://www.hq.nasa.gov/office/codef/workforce).*

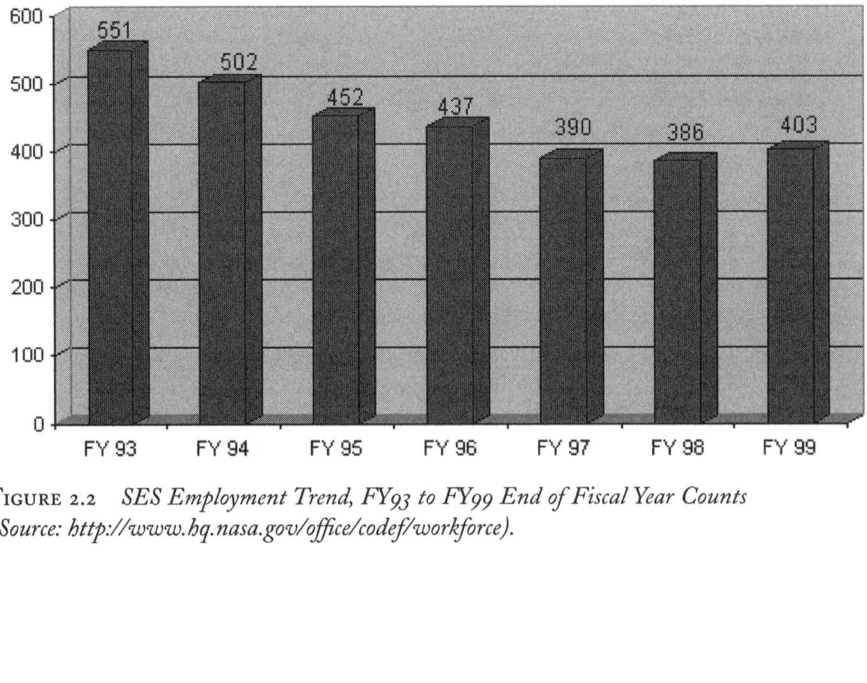


FIGURE 2.2 *SES Employment Trend, FY93 to FY99 End of Fiscal Year Counts (Source: http://www.hq.nasa.gov/office/codef/workforce).*

**Senior Executive Service**
Average Age Trend by Installation, FY 93 to FY 99
As of end of Fiscal Year

| | FY 93 | FY 94 | FY 95 | FY 96 | FY 97 | FY 98 | FY 99 |
|---|---|---|---|---|---|---|---|
| HQ | 53.0 | 50.4 | 51.7 | 52.6 | 52.0 | 51.7 | 51.4 |
| ARC | 54.4 | 55.1 | 55.6 | 56.3 | 54.4 | 53.3 | 52.5 |
| DFRC | --- | 57.4 | 58.5 | 55.4 | 55.9 | 55.8 | 55.9 |
| LARC | 55.0 | 54.1 | 53.1 | 54.6 | 55.1 | 55.6 | 55.3 |
| GRC | 55.9 | 55.0 | 53.8 | 53.2 | 51.8 | 52.4 | 52.9 |
| GSFC | 55.7 | 55.9 | 55.2 | 55.0 | 54.4 | 54.1 | 54.9 |
| MSFC | 57.5 | 51.8 | 57.2 | 56.6 | 56.0 | 56.0 | 54.4 |
| SSC | 56.1 | 56.8 | 50.2 | 51.2 | 52.2 | 54.3 | 51.7 |
| JSC | 54.9 | 55.2 | 54.8 | 54.3 | 54.9 | 54.5 | 53.6 |
| SSPO | --- | 49.0 | 47.9 | --- | --- | --- | --- |
| KSC | 56.4 | 55.7 | 55.0 | 56.4 | 52.3 | 51.7 | 51.8 |
| NASA IG | --- | 50.2 | 60.0 | 52.0 | 53.3 | 50.0 | 47.8 |
| NASA | 54.6 | 52.8 | 53.7 | 54.2 | 53.8 | 53.5 | 53.1 |

Notes: 1. Headquarters includes the Office of Inspector General for years prior to FY 1994.
2. Dryden employees are included with Ames employees prior to FY 1994.
3. SSPO was established during FY 1994, disestablished during FY 1996

Figure 2.3 *Senior Executive Service (Source: http://www.hq.nasa.gov/office/codef/workforce).*

Centers must still downsize. Hiring is very restricted at those Centers" (http://www.hq.nasa.gov/office/codef/workforce). The 16,742 losses in NASA full-time permanent (FTP) and other positions from FY1993 through June 27, 2002 are shown in the following statistics (*http://naade02.msfc.nasa.gov/cgi-bin/ppdscgi.exe?XT=losses*):

| | |
|---|---|
| FTP: | 11,042 persons |
| Other Non-FTP: | 2,882 |
| COOP: | 2,021 |
| Temporary/Term: | 615 |
| Part-Time Permanent: | 182 |

The NASA hires in these categories from FY1993 through October 5, 2002 was 11,305 hires. There were 4,928 buyouts during FY1994 through FY2001. As of the end of FY2002, the head count of all employee types of NASA federal civilians across the agency was 18,130 people, with 18.5 average years of federal service (http://naade02.msfc.nasa.gov/cgi-bin/ppdscgi.exe?XT=status_current).

The American Institute for Aeronautics and Astronautics (AIAA) states the following (http://www.aiaa.org/about/index.hfm?abo=280):

> *The Federal Government is not hiring and retaining an adequate number of freshouts from the Nation's key research and engineering universities—the government is no longer seen as an employer of choice by our most talented students. The existing technical workforce of the federal government is "graying" and we have a significant number of civil servants in key technical slots who are eligible to retire. The federal government appears unable to attract key talent from the private sector to serve in key science and technology management slots due to federal requirements on the transition of personnel from the private sector to the government and back.*

In order to move NASA to the "green" color on the Human Capital Scorecard, Judy Tenney, of NASA's Strategic Management and Planning Division, mentioned in a May 2002 briefing that the standards to get to "green" are (http://nodis.hq.nasa.gov/dir_homepage/jtenney.ppt):

- Human capital strategy aligned with mission, strategic goals, budget, and scorecards
- Citizen-centered structure
- High-performance workforce with flexibility to adapt to change
- No skill gaps in mission-critical areas
- Performance incentives linked to mission success
- Human capital solutions using existing flexibilities, tools, technology, and competitive sourcing

Tenney indicated that some of the corrective action needed for NASA to move toward the "green" direction were:

—Develop a comprehensive, integrated, and agile Agency Human Capital Strategic Plan

—Align with NASA mission and goals
—Help navigate through major human capital challenges
—Incorporate strategies, tactics, and metrics
—Integrate with other President's Management Agenda initiatives

NASA is trying hard to move towards the "green" strategic management of human capital. As Tenney points out, the following progress is being made:

- NASA has developed a Strategic Human Capital Plan Architecture and Agency-Wide Human Capital Strategy.
- There is improved use of existing recruitment and retention tools, networks, and so on.
- NASA is pursuing civil service legislative reforms through NASA Authorization Act 2002.
- NASA implemented a paperless hiring and promotion system.
- NASA has an enhanced program management training.

Other agencies are moving in similar directions as those at NASA in order to minimize the ensuing human capital crisis in their respective civilian workforces.

## Industry Is Also Experiencing Similar Human Capital Challenges

According to Angela Gonzales' *Business Journal* article "Employers Beware, Labor Shortages Loom Ahead" (October 18, 2002), the United States is facing a shortage of workers in the coming years. Gonzales states that the U.S. Bureau of Labor Statistics projections report that by 2010 there will be 168 million skilled jobs to fill in the United States. However, there only will be 158 million people in the workforce to fill those jobs. The large number of retirees will not be replaced by the upcoming generation in the workforce.

A number of important industries are being hit hard. According to META Group's *2002 IT (Information Technology) Staffing and Compensation Guide*, respondents from more than 600 medium-sized to large American corporations reported surprisingly high voluntary departure rates—over 10 percent. The META Group indicates that a turnover rate below 10 percent is relatively healthy, while higher than 10 percent turnover generally indicates an organization with fundamental issues that affect productivity and morale. The highest voluntary departure rates were reported in the transportation and distribution industry (20 percent), followed by media/publishing (18 percent) and healthcare (17 percent). According to the survey, the causes cited most commonly were economic conditions (33 percent), organizational restructuring (18 percent), and available skills (18 percent) (http://www.recruiter.com/052002_pr_it_1.cfm).

In a July 11, 2002 briefing titled "Creating Long-Term Value for the Boeing Company," prepared by the International Association of Machinists (IAM) Strategic Resources and SPEEA Research (http://www.goiam.org/publications/boeingcreatingvalue.ppt), Boeing's long-term competitive advantage depends on *human capital* and physical capacity. In recent years, there has been cost-cutting, shedding of assets, and outsourcing. In addition, a human capital challenge exists throughout the aerospace industry due to attrition (retirements, resignations, layoffs), failure to attract and retain new people, and loss of accumulated skills, knowledge, and experience. Boeing's employment levels in recent years is shown in Figure 2.4.

According to the IAM/SPEEA briefing, aerospace employment has been reduced by half in the last decade, from 1.2 million workers to about 500,000 workers. In the next decade, we are projected to lose 250,000 more jobs in the aerospace field. Also, there is an eroding industrial base and an aging and shrinking engineering and manufacturing community. Boeing hopes to leverage its competitive advantage to create value, but there are significant human capital challenges facing them and many others in the aerospace and transportation industries. Margaret Blair and Thomas Kochan, in their edited book,

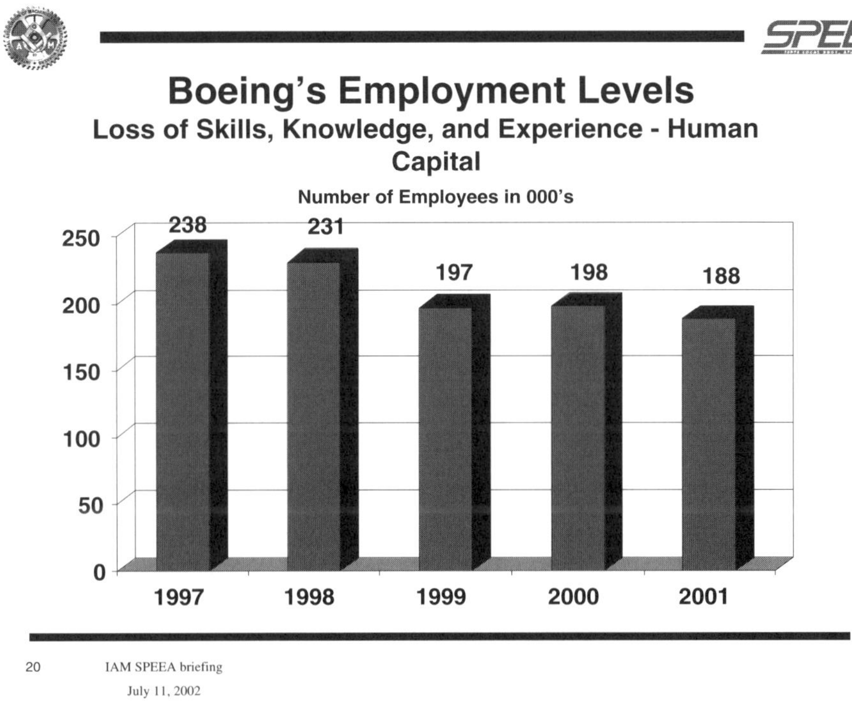


FIGURE 2.4 *Boeing's Employment Levels*
*(Source: http://www.goiam.org/publications/boeingcreatingvalue.ppt).*

*The New Relationship: Human Capital in the American Corporation* (Brookings Institution Press, 2000), stress that human capital is the key asset for competitive advantage in American businesses. Additionally, Mark Abramson and Nicole Gardner's edited book, *Human Capital 2002*, published by the PricewaterhouseCoopers Endowment for the Business of Government, highlights these ensuing human capital crises facing American government and businesses.

## ARE OTHER GOVERNMENTS EXPERIENCING SIMILAR HUMAN CAPITAL CRISES?

The United States government is not alone in experiencing human capital challenges. Other foreign governments have the same concerns. For example, according to the Advisory Committee on Senior Level Retention and Compensation Report, senior level federal Public Service employees in Canada face a human capital crisis as the demographics suggest that retirements alone will create a significant resource gap. By 2010, just over 80 percent of the federal executive community in Canada will be eligible to retire without actuarial reduction of their pension (http://dsp-psd.communication.gc.ca/Collection/BT43-104-2000E.pdf). In a May 2002 presentation by Irene Lewis, CEO of SAIT Canada, at the Chamber of Commerce in Alberta, Canada, Lewis mentioned a study conducted by the Canadian Federation of Independent Business that found that labor shortages continue to plague small and medium-sized businesses throughout Canada—approximately 265,000 jobs are currently vacant in the small business sector, and roughly 185,000 of them have been open for at least four months. According to Lewis, the national population increase is the lowest five-year growth rate in Canada's history. And with an aging workforce, there will be critical human capital shortages in Canada. Other countries throughout the world are also experiencing a shortage of federal civil servants in their respective governments.

## So, What Is Being Done about It?

In the United States, legislation has been recently introduced to address these human capital concerns in the federal workforce. On June 20, 2002, the Federal Workforce Improvement Act of 2002 was introduced by Senator Voinovich and others. Per the Public Hearings of The National Commission on the Public Service on July 18, 2002, at the Brookings Institution in Washington, D.C., Senator Voinovich discussed the main provisions of the bill, namely:

- Mandate chief human capital officers at all federal agencies to raise the institutional profile of human capital and better integrate agencies' workforce management with agency mission.

- Require the Office of Personnel Management to design a set of systems, including metrics for assessing agency's human capital management, and require agencies to include human capital strategic planning in their Government Performance and Results Acts (GPRA) report.
- Codify the Human Resources Management Council as the chief human capital officers council, an interagency advisory and coordinating working group, in order to share human capital best practices.
- Improve hiring procedures by authorizing agencies to use category ranking systems, based on an applicant's skills and experience.
- Authorize the use of voluntary separation incentive pay of up to $25,000 and voluntary early retirement in executive and judicial branch agencies for the purpose of workforce shaping.
- Offer agencies new flexibility in the use of relocation and retention bonuses, tools that can make a real difference in recruiting and retaining top candidates.
- Require agencies to link training activities with performance plans, appoint training officers to institute and oversee comprehensive management succession programs to develop future leaders, and provide special training to managers to deal with poor performers.
- Lift the current statutory restriction on payment for academic training.
- Offer better leave provisions for new federal employees hired at the mid-career level with several years of outside experience.
- Simplify and streamline the process for implementing management demonstration projects (i.e., to encourage agencies to experiment with new personnel systems). Lift the

caps on the number of employees per project and the number of projects permitted at any given time. Extend the demonstration period from five to ten years.

In the same Public Hearing on July 18, 2002, Representative Connie Morella (who has been a strong supporter of addressing the human capital problems in the federal workforce and introduced the Human Capital Bill HR 4580 in the U.S. House of Representatives) mentioned that recruitment and training are especially important factors in resolving the human capital crisis. According to Representative Morella, only 29 percent of nonfederal workers say they are well informed about federal government opportunities, and only 21 percent of college graduates polled in a survey recall a federal recruiter ever visiting their campus (http://www.brook.edu/comm/transcripts/20020718.pdf). Representative Morella also discussed the effects of downsizing and outsourcing in the government:

> *At the Social Security Administration between* 1982 *and* 2001, *the number of employees in regional and field offices, telephone service centers, and program service centers fell by* 28 *percent. The number of managers and supervisors in those frontline offices was cut in half. More than* 90 *percent of almost* 2,200 *Social Security Administration field managers surveyed said that management and staff cuts have seriously harmed its ability to manage itself and deliver high quality services to citizens. At the same time, the agency's workload is skyrocketing. The errors occurring now, such as overpaying, are a direct result of the agency cutting layers of manager and supervisors without changing business processes and practices. (http://www.brook.edu/comm/transcripts/*20020718*.pdf)*

Representative Morella is not saying that downsizing should not be done in the federal government; rather, she strongly suggests that there should be a clear plan, policy, and strategy for any personnel cuts. Morella suggests revamping the federal pay system to possibly develop a pay-sharing system that would reward units as opposed to individuals and enhance teamwork and recognition within federal agencies for successful work. Here many of the basic tenets of knowledge management and knowledge sharing are being promoted.

Certainly, it seems clear that a human capital strategy needs to be developed for each federal agency. There are many challenges ahead to resolve the human capital crisis in the federal workforce. The next chapter will help by describing a methodology and model for building such a human capital strategy.

# THREE
# Developing a Human Capital Strategy

In the first two chapters we discussed human capital, its role in the federal government, and the ensuing federal human capital crisis. We now turn to how to develop a human capital strategy for a federal agency. Within the past year, several human capital strategy models have been presented by various U.S. federal agencies, as Brian Friel points out in his *Government Executive* article "Reality Check" (May 15, 2002):

- As part of the Bush administration's management agenda, the OMB (Office of Management and Budget) and the Office of Personnel Management (OPM) issued a human capital scorecard using red, yellow, and green lights to rate agencies on their strategic management of human capital.
- The governmentwide Human Resources Management Council developed a scorecard that covers more specific measures than does the OMB scorecard, including training effectiveness, diversity, recruitment and retention targets, and distribution of workers to frontline service positions rather than to backend administration jobs.
- The General Accounting Office produced a "maturity model" that agencies can use to measure themselves on a three-level scale for eight factors.

- OPM developed a 113-question survey about employees' satisfaction with workforce management at their agencies.

Bush's fiscal 2003 budget proposal assigned red lights to human resources management at all but three agencies: the Social Security Administration, Labor Department, and OPM got yellow lights (http://207.27.3.29/features/fpp/fpp02/s3.htm). Most U.S. federal agencies have quite a way to go in order to improve their human capital strategic management rating to green. Some of the questions to consider for rating are (http://207.27.3.29/features/fpp/fpp02/s3.htm):

- Does the agency have sufficient numbers of people with the right skills and abilities to carry out the mission?
- Is the agency able to allocate its personnel, by mission or geographically, in a way that maximizes its ability to achieve its mission?
- Does the agency engage in workforce planning that is designed to determine future human resource requirements, and are employees and stakeholders involved in these planning efforts?
- To what extent does the agency provide line managers with the capability to hire, fire, reward, and train the people who work for them?

Human capital is the key strategic asset to an organization. In the private sector, human capital has been directly linked to shareholder value. According to the Watson Wyatt Research Report on Human Capital Index, superior human capital practices are not only correlated with financial returns; they are, in fact, a leading indicator of increased shareholder value (http://www.watsonwyatt.com/research). The key message is that if a company's goal is to improve shareholder value, a key priority must be its approach to human capital. The results from the Watson Wyatt's 2001 Human Capital Index study of more than 750 North American companies and 250 European companies indicate that the better an organization is doing in managing its human capital, the better its returns for shareholders. Those in the low group averaged a 21 percent five-year return; the medium group averaged 39 percent; the high Human Capital Index scores returned 64 percent over five years. The study also showed that a significant improvement in 43 key human resources practices is associated with an increase of 47 percent in market value. The key links between human capital and shareholder value creation are shown in the following table:

| PRACTICE | *IMPACT ON MARKET VALUE* |
|---|---|
| Total rewards and accountability | 16.5% |
| Collegial, flexible workplace | 9.0% |
| Recruiting and retention excellence | 7.9% |
| Communication integrity | 7.1% |
| Focused HR service technologies | 6.5% |

From this study, it appears that the evidence clearly favors human capital practices as a *leading* indicator of business success.

Highlights of the conference notes from "The 2001 Human Capital Summit on Recruitment and Retention for Government Agencies (July 19–20, 2001)," prepared by Boni Bigornia with the Recruitment Task Force, suggest that the U.S. federal agencies have a variety of recruitment and retention strategies as part of their overall human capital strategy. For example, the Forest Service now has a workforce plan and a five-year recruiting strategy. In the past, their workforce planning was not linked with their strategy and budget, and there was no recruiting coordination. At the Social Security Administration, every employee is supposed to have a mentor. The Treasury Department offers "shadow days" to help mentor new employees.

## WHAT HUMAN CAPITAL STRATEGY MODELS AND MEASURES ARE AVAILABLE IN THE FEDERAL GOVERNMENT?

According to the testimony of David Walker, U.S. Comptroller General, "Using Strategic Human Capital Management to Drive

Transformational Change" (July 15, 2002 before the National Commission on the Public Service), federal agencies need to transform their cultures and shift their overall orientation from (GAO Report 02-940T):

- Processes to results
- Stovepipes to matrixes
- Hierarchical to flatter and more horizontal structures
- An inward focus to an external (citizen, customer, and stakeholder) focus
- Management control to employee empowerment
- Reactive behavior to proactive approaches
- Avoiding new technologies to embracing and leveraging them
- Hoarding knowledge to sharing knowledge
- Avoiding risk to managing risk
- Protecting turf to forming partnerships

Coincidentally, many of these goals form the basic tenets for **knowledge management.** On April 12, 2001, David Walker gave a presentation entitled "Human Capital and Knowledge Management: Connecting People to Information." In his talk, Walker highlighted how knowledge management assists human capital management (http://www.gao.gov/cghome/km):

- Supports matrix management (i.e., with mechanisms to bring the right people with the right skills together to maximize the value and manage risk involved with any undertaking);
- Aids coordination across borders, sectors, agencies, levels, and boundaries;
- Helps leaders and employees embrace needed cultural transformations;
- Helps leaders manage change;
- Helps managers plan their IT efforts to support employee's knowledge sharing needs;

- Helps employees identify their efforts to their organization's strategic plan by assisting in building expertise, enhancing professional development, improving recruitment, and improving retention.

For many of these reasons, knowledge management can be seen as a key pillar of an organization's human capital strategy.

In April 2001, the American Society for Training and Development issued recommendations on improving the human capital management in the federal government. One of the recommendations was to encourage agencies to develop a learning strategy that includes e-learning as a key component for maximizing technology for customized, anytime, anywhere learning. Developing a learning strategy should be a critical part of an agency's human capital strategy. According to Professor Ian Cunningham in the United Kingdom (http://www.selfmanagedlearning.org), a good learning strategy should include the following:

- Change strategies need to include reference to learning needs that will be part of the change (i.e., a learning strategy has to be part of a change process).
- Learning has to be seen as an organizationwide commitment, managed from the top and highly visible.
- Much learning cannot be achieved through quick-fix modes.
- Other people management practices need to tie in with a learning strategy.
- Shared learning needs encouragement.

David Skyrme, in his article "Developing a Knowledge Strategy" (http://www.skyrme.com/pubs/knwstrat.htm), believes that learning is an important component of a "knowledge strategy" as well. A knowledge strategy typically has two thrusts. The first is to make better use of the knowledge that already exists within the firm. The second major thrust of knowledge-focused strategies is innovation—

the creation of new knowledge and turning ideas into valuable products and services (http://www.skyrme.com/pubs/knwstrat.htm). Here, transforming individualized learning into organizational learning is critical.

On March 15, 2002, GAO released "Model of Strategic Human Capital Management" (GAO Report 02-373SP) that agencies could follow. This model has four human capital cornerstones, eight critical success factors, and three levels of measurement. The model is shown in the following table:

| *HUMAN CAPITAL CORNERSTONES* | *CRITICAL SUCCESS FACTORS* |
|---|---|
| Leadership | • Commitment to human capital management<br>• Role of the human capital function |
| Strategic human capital planning | • Integration and alignment<br>• Data-driven human capital decisions |
| Acquiring, developing, and retaining talent | • Targeted investments in people<br>• Human capital approaches tailored to meet organizational needs |
| Results-oriented organizational cultures | • Empowerment and inclusiveness<br>• Unit and individual performance linked to organizational goals |

Each of the critical success factors can be described in three levels, as discussed in GAO Report 02-373SP:

**Level 1:** The approach to human capital is largely compliance-based; the agency has yet to realize the value of managing human capital strategically to achieve results; existing human capital approaches have yet to be assessed in light of current and emerging agency needs.

**Level 2:** The agency recognizes that people are a critical asset that must be managed strategically; new human capital policies, programs, and practices are being designed and implemented to support mission accomplishment.

**Level 3:** The agency's human capital approaches contribute to improved agency performance; human capital considerations are fully integrated into strategic planning and day-to-day operations; the agency is continuously seeking ways to further improve its people management to achieve results.

Besides the GAO model for human capital, OPM (through the Human Resources Management Council) has a Human Capital Scorecard that considers five areas as key dimensions of human capital: Strategic Alignment, Strategic Competencies (Talent), Leadership, Performance Culture (Strategic Awareness), and Learning (Knowledge Management). The following tables outline the performance goals and measures under each of these five dimensions (http://www.opm.gov/humancapital/scorecard.htm):

**Strategic Alignment:** Align human capital policies to support the accomplishment of the agency's mission, vision, goals, and strategies (which define its direction and its expectations for itself and its people).

| *Performance Goals* | *Measures* |
|---|---|
| There is an explicit and well-communicated link between HR strategies and plans and the agencies' strategic objectives | • Agency has documented links between HR strategy and plans with mission/program objectives.<br>• Agency has effective process for communicating the link between HR strategies and plans with mission/program objectives. |
| The organization is well structured to support its mission | • Agency has effective restructuring and organizational deployment plans and is taking actions based on them. The standard for "effective" is deploying the appropriate workforce mix to get the job done. |
| Employees understand their organization's plans and are involved in the strategic planning and reporting process | • Employees understand how their job fits in and contributes to fulfilling the agency mission. |

**Strategic Competencies (Talent):** Recruit, hire, develop, and retain employees with the strategic competencies for mission critical occupations.

| *Performance Goals* | *Measures* |
|---|---|
| Desired competency levels in mission-critical occupations is achieved | • Agency meets gap-reduction targets developed from restructuring plans. |
| Desired recruitment/retention rate for employees with strategic competencies is achieved | • Agency meets staffing/retention rate targets for employees with strategic competencies. |
| Desired quality level of new hires is achieved | • Agency meets quality-level targets for new hires. |

**Leadership:** Ensures that leadership in the agency inspires, motivates, and guides others towards goals; coaches, mentors, challenges staff; adapts leadership styles to various situations; models high standards of honesty, integrity, trust, openness, and respect for individuals by applying these values.

| *Performance Goals* | *Measures* |
|---|---|
| Agency recruits, develops, and retains high performing leaders | • Agency meets staffing/retention target for high-performing executives and managers.<br>• Agency has effective plans for leadership recruitment (including identifying potential leaders from within the organizations). development, and succession that include specific objectives, actions, and timetables, and an analysis of candidate pools.<br>• Agency creates a culture in which employees believe that they are encouraged to assume more responsibilities and to accept assignments that provide leadership opportunities. |
| Agency leaders create high levels of motivation and commitment in the workforce | • Employees are focused on results and show interest in improving the services of their organization. |
| Leaders maintain high standards of honesty and integrity that serve as a model to the whole workforce | • Employees hold their leaders in high regard. |

**Performance Culture (Strategic Awareness):** Create a culture that motivates employees for high performance, based on their contribution to the work of the organization, and common values while ensuring fairness in the workplace.

| *Performance Goals* | *Measures* |
|---|---|
| Agency develops, rewards, and retains high performers and deals effectively with poor performers | • Agency has effective performance management system that adequately distinguishes between levels of performance.<br>• Employees believe that their performance is valued by the organization for its contribution to fulfilling the agency's missions.<br>• Agency effectively manages employees who are performing below expectations. |
| Employees are engaged and focused on achieving the results expected of them | • Employees believe that their organization has set high but realistic results-oriented work expectations for them. |
| Agency fosters a climate that values diversity | • Employees believe that differences are welcomed and contribute to the work of the organization.<br>• Agency sets realistic diversity goals and targets and is meeting them. |

**Learning (Knowledge Management):** Promote a knowledge-sharing culture and a climate of openness; promote continuous learning and improvement.

| *Performance Goals* | *Measures* |
|---|---|
| Knowledge management strategies and/or systems are in place | • Agency has effective strategy for knowledge management with targeted objectives and defined results. |
| Agency invests strategically in training and development opportunities for employees | • Agency strategies include investment assumptions and cost-benefit analyses for training and development opportunities. |
| A climate of learning and growth exists throughout the agency | • Employees believe that their organization supports their development and expects them to improve their skills and learn new skills to do their jobs better. |

In November 2002, OPM, OMB, and GAO decided to combine their work into a comprehensive human capital framework. This framework is called the "Human Capital Assessment and Accountability Framework" and consists of the following:

| *Human Capital Standard for Success* | *Critical Success Factor* |
|---|---|
| Strategic Alignment | • Human capital focus<br>• Government-wide human capital collaboration<br>• Human resources collaboration |
| Workforce Planning and Deployment | • Workforce planning<br>• Workforce deployment |
| Leadership and Knowledge Management | • Leadership planning and implementation (Senior Executive Service, Managers, and Supervisors)<br>• Change management<br>• Integrity and inspiring employee commitment<br>• Strategic knowledge management<br>• Continuous learning and improvement |
| Performance Culture | • Performance management<br>• Diversity<br>• Employee/labor–management relations |
| Talent | • Workforce analysis<br>• Competition for talent |
| Accountability | • Agencywide system for ensuring accountability in human capital |

## An Agency Developing Its Human Capital Strategy: The Internal Revenue Service

Napoleon Avery, Deputy Chief Human Resource Officer at the Internal Revenue Service (IRS), gave a briefing on "Strategic Human Capital Management" in June 2002. In his talk he mentioned that the strategic management of human capital must be achieved due to looming retirements and skill imbalances, and to reduce layers between citizens and decision-makers, better align skills, and provide greater flexibility to acquire and develop talent and leadership (www.psc-cfp.gc.ca/conf2002/presentations/ avery_strategic_hrm.ppt). The human capital strategy for the Internal Revenue Service is organized around four strategic human resources (HR) imperatives: renewal, investment, performance, and transition. In turn, the HR life cycle of the IRS is plan, recruit, educate, develop, sustain, and transition. According to Avery, the center of the IRS approach is the human resources strategy and structure. Currently, the IRS has a new decentralized HR organization structure and governance mechanisms, strategic partnerships (with senior leadership team and union), HR staff renewal, strategic measures and evaluation, and an HRIS (Human Resources Information System) strategy. The IRS plans on heading toward process reengineering, PeopleSoft implementation (HR Connect), and career development strategy for HR professionals.

In terms of the "Plan" function in the HR life cycle, the IRS is heading towards an integrated workforce planning tool, leadership succession plan, and annual strategic HR plan. Under "Recruit," the IRS is going towards direct-hire for critical skills and mid/senior level recruiting strategy. For "Educate," the IRS is heading towards online course repository (competency-based) and curriculum, e-learning investment fund, continuing curriculum redesign (high-tech/high-touch), and advanced learning technology acquisition vehicle. Under "Develop," the IRS wants career management systems for mission-critical occupations, frontline/senior manager readiness programs, and university leadership training. For "Sustain," the IRS is moving towards payband expansion, new bargaining unit appraisal system, seasonal employee health benefits, SES (Senior Executive Service) demonstration project, cafeteria health benefits plan, and elder care subsidies. For "Transition," phased retirement and web-based change management training are being proposed. Thus the IRS, with its five-year Strategic HR Strategy, is striving to achieve the "best-in-class" status in strategic HR in the following areas (www.psc-cfp.gc.ca/conf2002/presentations/ avery_strategic_hrm.ppt ):

- Treat HR as fundamental to strategic management
- Integrate HR staff into top management team
- Leverage external partnerships
- Hire, develop, and sustain leaders based on competencies
- Communicate a shared vision
- Hire, develop, and retain employees based on competencies
- Use meaningful performance management systems
- Support and reward teams
- Use employee input
- Measure effectiveness

## Developing an Approach for Constructing a Human Capital Strategy

Having a methodology or process to develop a human capital strategy is essential. It is similar to the strategic planning process that shapes and results in the organization's strategic plan. For example, the steps in the knowledge management methodology are to identify knowledge, capture knowledge, share knowledge, apply knowledge, and create knowledge. Ultimately, based on these steps, a knowledge management strategy is developed that could include systematically capturing critical knowledge, creating a unified knowledge network, and strengthening incentives to reuse knowledge for building and nurturing a knowledge sharing culture.

What steps, process, or methodology should be followed to create a human capital strategy? The first step is to understand the organization's strategy, goals, values, and guiding principles to be sure that the human capital strategy is in direct alignment with the organization's strategy, mission, and vision. Next, a crossfunctional team may be created to develop the human capital strategy. The chair of the team could be the human resources director, chief human capital officer, chief knowledge officer, strategic planning officer, or the like. Once the team is assembled, a data collection effort should commence to collect relevant organizational documents, plans, policies, guidelines, and studies that may be pertinent to the human capital strategic effort. Additionally, benchmarking what other comparable organizations have done in the human capital arena and identifying best practices in human capital strategic planning from industry, government, and academe should be accomplished. Then, employee surveys and focus groups with relevant stakeholders (e.g., employees, management, retirees, unions, etc.) should be conducted. Based upon this input, a draft human capital strategy should be developed and should be briefed to senior management or a human capital steering committee for their input. The human capital strategy and plan should then be revised and presented to various stakeholders throughout the organization for their feedback. Once accomplished, the final version of the human capital strategy and plan should be made and briefed to the executive council of the organization, to be followed by presentations to "all-hands" in the organization.

NASA Goddard Space Flight Center (GSFC) had a well-organized approach for developing its human capital strategy. A human capital working group (HCWG), comprised of representatives across the directorates, was chartered by the center director to develop the human capital strategy for GSFC. A human capital steering committee, made up of representatives from the executive council, was formed in which the HCWG shared and consulted with the steering committee. An outside consulting firm, well-versed in developing human capital strategies for the government, also helped in guiding the HCWG. Weekly meetings of the HCWG were held, then an extensive data collection effort was undertaken. A working definition for human capital was developed and agreed to by the HCWG, human capital steering committee, executive council, and center director. Existing human resource and workforce planning studies previously conducted at GSFC, as well as documents and presentations of agency-related human capital efforts, were gathered and reviewed. Interim briefings on the status of the HCWG's progress were given by the HCWG to the human capital steering committee and executive council. Focus groups, numbering eleven or so, were set up to get input on a draft human capital strategy from the various stakeholders at GSFC (e.g., GSFC engineers and scientists, professional and administrative employees, wage earners, employees at affiliated GSFC facilities, unions, etc.). This input from the focus groups helped to refine the human capital strategy, and then briefings were given to the center director, human capital steering committee, executive council, and all-hands.

Once the human capital strategy was developed and agreed to by those at GSFC, the next step entailed fleshing out the component parts of the strategy and then developing an implementation plan for the human capital strategy. In the next chapter, we will take a look at the necessary parts of such a human capital strategy.

# FOUR

# The Four Pillars of Human Capital

In the first three chapters we gained an appreciation and understanding of human capital and the ensuing human capital crisis in the U.S. federal government. We also learned about approaches for developing a human capital strategy and what various federal agencies are doing in this domain. Now, we turn to describing the essential components of a human capital strategy—that is, what we are calling the four pillars of human capital.

Before examining the underpinnings of a human capital strategy, let's first take a look at the general workplace environment in the United States. According to the U.S. Department of Labor, Americans are now working more hours, on average, than employees in any other industrialized nation. In an article titled "Take this Job and . . . " (*Johns Hopkins Magazine*, November 2002), Ed Bernacki, with the Department of Occupational Medicine at Johns Hopkins School of Medicine, indicates the following statistics:

- 24 percent of U.S. employees are putting in more than 50 hours per week
- 22 percent of U.S. employees work six and sometimes seven days per week
- 25 percent of U.S. employees never use their vacation time
- 40 percent of U.S. employees find their jobs "very" or "extremely" stressful

The message is that American workers today are more stressed out than ever before. Increased stress can lead to ill health and injury among workers, and reduced productivity. Additionally, high stress can affect the human capital assets in an organization.

Let's look at other statistics regarding the American labor force. The following tables were developed by the Office of Occupational Statistics and Employment Projections at the U.S. Bureau of Labor Statistics (http://stats.bls.gov/emp/home.htm):

TABLE 4.1 *Distribution of the Population and Labor Force by Age and Sex, 2000 and Projected 2010 (Percent)*

| *Group* | *Population 2000* | *Population 2010* | *Labor Force 2000* | *Labor Force 2010* |
|---|---|---|---|---|
| Total, 16 years and older | 100.0 | 100.0 | 100.0 | 100.0 |
| —16 to 24 | 16.4 | 16.8 | 16.1 | 16.5 |
| —25 to 39 | 28.4 | 25.0 | 35.7 | 32.1 |
| —40 and over | 55.2 | 58.2 | 48.2 | 51.4 |
| —65 and over | 15.6 | 15.8 | 2.4 | 2.9 |
| —75 and over | 7.1 | 7.0 | 0.6 | 0.6 |
| Men, 16 years and older | 100.0 | 100.0 | 100.0 | 100.0 |
| —16 to 24 | 17.2 | 17.6 | 15.8 | 16.3 |
| —25 to 39 | 28.9 | 25.4 | 36.1 | 32.3 |
| —40 and over | 53.9 | 57.1 | 48.1 | 51.4 |
| —65 and over | 13.8 | 14.2 | 3.2 | 3.8 |
| —75 and over | 5.8 | 5.8 | 0.6 | 0.6 |

Table 4.1 (continued)

| *Group* | *Population* 2000 | *Population* 2010 | *Labor Force* 2000 | *Labor Force* 2010 |
|---|---|---|---|---|
| Women, 16 years and older | 100.0 | 100.0 | 100.0 | 100.0 |
| —16 to 24 | 15.7 | 16.1 | 16.5 | 16.8 |
| —25 to 39 | 27.8 | 24.6 | 35.2 | 31.8 |
| —40 and over | 56.4 | 59.3 | 48.3 | 51.4 |
| —65 and over | 17.2 | 17.3 | 2.7 | 3.1 |
| —75 and over | 8.3 | 8.0 | 0.5 | 0.5 |

Table 4.2 *Median Ages of the Labor Force, by Sex, Race, and Hispanic Origin, Selected Historical Years and Projected 2010*

| *Group* | *1962* | *1980* | *1990* | 2000 | 2010 |
|---|---|---|---|---|---|
| Total | 40.5 | 34.6 | 36.6 | 39.3 | 40.6 |
| Men | 40.5 | 35.1 | 36.7 | 39.3 | 40.6 |
| Women | 40.4 | 33.9 | 36.4 | 39.3 | 40.6 |
| White | 40.9 | 34.8 | 36.8 | 39.7 | 41.3 |
| Black | * | 33.3 | 34.9 | 37.3 | 37.7 |
| Asian and other** | * | 33.8 | 36.5 | 37.8 | 38.7 |
| Hispanic origin*** | **** | 30.7 | 33.2 | 34.9 | 36.4 |
| White non-Hispanic | **** | 35.0 | 37.0 | 40.4 | 42.2 |

*Data not available before 1972.
**The "Asian and other" group includes (1) Asians and Pacific Islanders and (2) American Indians and Alaska Natives. The historic data are derived by subtracting "Black" and "White" from the Total; projections are made directly.
***Persons of Hispanic origin may be of any race.
***Data not available before 1980.

Now that we have a sense for the distribution, race, and ages of the projected labor force in 2010 in the United States, we can use this data as background information for helping us shape a human capital strategy. Let's take a look at the essential pillars that should lay the foundation for a human capital strategy.

## THE ESSENTIALS OF A HUMAN CAPITAL STRATEGY

Various solutions have been proposed for partially resolving the government's human capital crisis. For example, David Walker, Comptroller General of the U.S., in his E-Gov 2001 speech entitled "Efforts to Address GAO's Human Capital Challenges," mentioned various legislative reforms that would need to be done, including broadbanding systems for mission staff, expected hiring authority (e.g., internship program), special pay rates, senior level for technical staff, targeted early-outs and buyout authority, revised reduction in force rules, and the like. Others concerned about the federal human capital crisis have discussed ways of bringing back retirees in knowledge retention and mentoring roles, and having programs where industry-government exchanges of personnel for some periods of time could be made. Whatever combination of human capital strategies is utilized, the underlying foundations should at least include the following:

- *Competency management:* What competencies/knowledge areas should the organization's workforce know?
- *Performance management:* How can these competencies be transformed into performance?
- *Knowledge management:* How can the institutional memory of the organization be built before employees leave the organization?
- *Change management:* What needs to be done, from a cultural viewpoint, to stimulate and achieve change in the organization?

According to the 2002 book *Competency Management in the Public Sector* (edited by S. Horton, D. Franham, and A. Hondeghem, IOS Press), competency management is increasingly being adopted as an approach to human resources management in both the private and public sectors. Much of the competency management movement can be traced from the 1980s in the United States and the United Kingdom. In the U.K., for example, a holistic approach to competency management in the Senior Civil Service is used, and there is also widespread use throughout the rest of the service. In France and Germany, however, competency management has just recently appeared on the reform agenda.

Competency-based management is being used in the Public Service of Canada. According to *The Framework for Competency-Based Management in the Public Service of Canada* (Treasury Board of Canada and the Public Service Commission, December 1999), competency-based management is the application of a set of competencies to the management of human resources to achieve both excellence in performance and results that are relevant to the organization's business strategies. Competencies refer to the knowledge, skills, abilities, and behaviors that an employee applies in performing his or her work. According to the Public Service Commission of Canada, competencies differ from qualifications because of the linking of competencies to the strategic objectives and capabilities of the organization, and because competencies can be used to track performance in all human resources areas (including training, development, performance management, and succession planning—not simply resourcing). Competency profiles can be developed as a set of competencies that includes associated behaviors that link directly to overall strategic priorities and the work that needs to be done to achieve them, as well as to levels of proficiency for each behavior (http://www.tbs-sct.gc.ca/hr_connexions_rh/sigs/CBHRM/framework_cbm/fcbm1_e.html).

In 1998, the Public Service Commission ran a study surveying fifty-seven organizations within the Canadian federal sector to determine the interest in and status of competency-based management. At that time, thirty-two organizations had launched competency-based projects for at least one human resource application. Many private sector companies have also followed suit. Companies using competency-based management approaches generally have (http://www.tbs-sct.gc.ca/hr_connexions_rh/sigs/CBHRM/framework_cbm/fcbm1_e.html):

- Based competencies on their corporate culture, values, and business strategies to enhance competitive advantage;
- Used the executives of the organization and the business mission and strategies as starting points for identifying a specific direction and consistency in applying competencies;
- Defined competencies in terms of how performance could be enhanced by applying job-specific skills and behaviors;
- Positioned competency-based management as part of an overall business strategy or change process, and not as a stand-alone end in itself;
- Integrated competencies into current human resource systems where the need was greatest, as opposed to revamping programs around competencies;
- Aligned actual behaviors with those behaviors that were valued in the organization.

Like competency management, performance management should play a critical role in an organization. In terms of performance management, the U.S. Office of Personnel Management (OPM) has defined performance management as the systematic process by which an agency involves its employees, as individuals and members of a group, in improving organizational effectiveness in the accomplishment of agency mission and goals (http://www.opm.gov/perform/overview.asp). According to OPM, employee performance management includes:

- **Planning** work and setting expectations (set goals and measures; establish and communicate elements and standards);
- Continually **monitoring** performance (measure performance; provide feedback; conduct progress review);
- **Developing** the capacity to perform (address poor performance; improve good performance);
- Periodically **rating** performance in a summary fashion (summarize performance; assign the rating of record);
- **Rewarding** good performance (recognize and reward good performance).

All five of these processes, working together, should achieve effective performance management.

OPM's *Handbook for Measuring Employee Performance: Aligning Employee Performance Plans with Organizational Goals* (Report PMD-013, September 2001) asserts how performance elements tell employees "what" they have to do and standards tell them "how well" they have to do it. One of the problems with the current employee performance plans in the U.S. government is that the performance elements are typically on a pass-fail scale. By using a pass-fail scale, little feedback is provided to the employee during the typical employee annual performance review. Besides employee performance, U.S. federal agencies are required to develop organizational performance plans under the Government Performance and Results Act (GPRA) of 1993 (OMB Circular A-11). These organizational performance plans:

- Establish program-level performance goals that are objective, quantifiable, and measurable;
- Describe the operational resources needed to meet those goals;
- Establish performance indicators to be used in measuring the outcomes of each program.

Senator Fred Thompson, Chairman of the Senate Governmental Affairs Committee, issued the Thompson Report that looked at how well the U.S. agencies are doing with respect to their organizational performance plans. Committee staff meetings with agency officials and the reviews of agency documents revealed that agencies have not consistently developed performance goals and associated measures that directly address their respective management challenges and high-risk programs (www.whitehouse.gov/omb/circulars/a11/2002). For fiscal year 2001 Performance Plans, "the Committee staff found that 11 of the 24 agencies reported few, if any, specific and readily identifiable goals and measures that directly address their major management problems. Eight of the 24 agencies reported a moderate level of such goals and measures for these management challenges. Only 5 of the 24 agencies reported more extensive goals and measures that directly address these challenges" (http://www.senate.gov/~gov_affairs/102700_Agency-Performance%20Goals.pdf; http://207.27.3.29/gpra/govaffairs/1000report/efforts.htm).

Besides performance management and competency management, knowledge management is a critical component of a human capital strategy. Nick Bontis and J. Fitzenz's article, "Intellectual Capital Return on Investment: A Causal Map of Human Capital Antecedents and Consequents" (*Journal of Intellectual Capital*, vol. 3, no. 3, Emerald, 2002), presents research that shows the importance of coupling knowledge management activities with general human resources policy. Knowledge management activities fall along three constructs: knowledge generation, knowledge integration, and knowledge sharing. Their research shows that employee commitment has a positive influence on knowledge generation and that knowledge sharing will occur if value alignment is evident. Thus, their research shows that knowledge management initiatives can decrease turnover rates and support business performance if they are coupled with human resources policies. This suggests that knowledge management and human capital have an important, intertwined role.

Knowledge management involves how best to leverage knowledge internally and externally. The knowledge management steps are typically knowledge identification, knowledge capture, knowledge sharing, knowledge application, and knowledge creation. Usually the Chief Knowledge Officer (CKO) is responsible for spearheading the knowledge management initiatives in an organization. According to Dr. Robert Neilson of the National Defense University and the Federal CIO Council's Subcommittee on Knowledge Management (http://www.fgipc.org/02_Federal_CIO_Council/cko.htm), the role of a CKO in a public sector organization involves focusing the CKO's efforts on an integrated set of activities that address organizational behaviors, processes, and technologies. Dr. Neilson feels that the six competency areas that public sector CKOs should possess include leadership and management, communications, strategic thinking, tools and technologies, personal behaviors, and personal knowledge and cognitive capability (in fact, these competency areas probably hold true for CKOs in the private sector). In Michael Mitchell and Nick Bontis' article "A CKO's Raison D'Etre: Driving Value-Based Performance Gains by Aligning Human Capital with Business Strategy" (January 14, 2000; http://mint.mcmaster.ca/mint/papers/papers.htm), Mitchell and Bontis feel that there are many tools to help CKOs achieve alignment strategies that fill human capital gaps, and that a CKO must be well-oriented to human resources management, IT management, and strategic management. Many organizations use knowledge management to retain key expertise—that is, to preserve the human and intellectual capital in the organization. Thus, knowledge management needs to play a central role in a human capital strategy.

Various knowledge roles for those in an organization can be developed to further support the organization's knowledge management activities and human capital strategy. Michael Berens and the author of this text developed a set of knowledge roles for those at the American Society for Interior Designers. These are shown in the following table:

| | *Director* | *Professional* | *Admin/Support* |
|---|---|---|---|
| ***KNOWLEDGE ROLES*** **(Adapted from J. Liebowitz and M. Berens work at ASID)** | | | |
| KNOWLEDGE IDENTIFICATION & CAPTURE | | | |
| Identify Knowledge | • Identify areas of knowledge that the organization needs to capture.<br>• Identify knowledge and knowledge competencies needed to accomplish strategic goals.<br>• Identify knowledge deliverables from major projects or efforts. | • Identify sources for capturing knowledge as assigned.<br>• Identify emerging issues/trends within or affecting assigned organizational segments. | • Alert staff to urgent and emerging service issues. |
| Capture Knowledge | • Establish policies for managing knowledge and quality standards for knowledge work.<br>• Establish schedules for knowledge capture and reporting.<br>• Monitor knowledge contributions of assigned staff for quality and frequency. | • Monitor knowledge sources and compile relevant knowledge as assigned.<br>• Capture lessons learned and successful practices from major projects and make them available on the intranet.<br>• Monitor and collect information from chat rooms and threaded discussions to help identify issues for future research, online communities, and product/service offerings. | • Record and compile job-related data and information as assigned.<br>• Report lessons learned and successful practices.<br>• Post on the intranet and update as necessary relevant information and documentation for operating unit, as assigned. |

| | *Director* | *Professional* | *Admin/Support* |
|---|---|---|---|
| KNOWLEDGE SHARING | | | |
| **Communicate Knowledge** | • Facilitate open communication and knowledge sharing throughout the organization.<br>• Provide key stakeholders with regular updates/ progress reports on major projects.<br>• Ensure that others receive timely and useful communiqués of information and knowledge they need to perform. | • Provide key stakeholders with regular updates/progress reports on major projects/efforts.<br>• Ensure that others receive timely and useful communiqués of information and knowledge they need to perform effectively. | • Ensure that others receive timely and useful communiqués of information and knowledge they need to perform effectively. |
| **Build and Nurture a Knowledge Sharing Culture** | • Establish crossfunctional project teams and foster collaboration.<br>• Recognize and reward knowledge sharing, creation, and use.<br>• Encourage and facilitate in-time, on-the-job learning and skills transfer.<br>• Practice and promote knowledge sharing across the enterprise. | • Establish or participate in communities of interest, communities of practice, or other informal knowledge sharing groups.<br>• Respond promptly to requests for knowledge or subject matter expertise, making sure that the response meets the requestor's need.<br>• Acknowledge when others share knowledge. | • Respond promptly to requests for knowledge or subject matter expertise, making sure that the response meets the requestor's need.<br>• Acknowledge when others share knowledge. |

| | *Director* | *Professional* | *Admin/Support* |
|---|---|---|---|
| KNOWLEDGE APPLICATION | | | |
| **Incorporate Knowledge** | • Adjust strategy as needed, based on emerging knowledge.<br>• Ground decision-making in explicit knowledge.<br>• Review evaluations of products, services, and programs periodically, and adjust offerings accordingly. | • Gather relevant knowledge objects and assemble necessary expertise to achieve project goals.<br>• Look for ways to add and use new knowledge to existing or new products, services, or programs.<br>• Recommend modifications to projects or tasks, when needed, based on emerging knowledge.<br>• Contribute suggestions for new products, services, and process improvements. | • Recommend modifications to procedures or tasks, when needed, based on emerging knowledge.<br>• Contribute suggestions for new products, services, and process improvements. |
| **Reuse Knowledge** | • Maintain and refer to "organizational memory" of how strategy was set or decisions reached. | • Consult intranet and other knowledge resources to review lessons learned and proven practices when undertaking new projects and efforts.<br>• Use templates and other preformatted materials. | • Use templates and other preformatted materials. |

| | *Director* | *Professional* | *Admin/Support* |
|---|---|---|---|
| KNOWLEDGE CREATION | | | |
| **Create Knowledge** | • Communicate, reinforce, and clearly link to projects and activities the organization's vision, mission, and goals, to provide context for knowledge application and learning.<br>• Identify and synthesize key learnings and report to leadership. | • Analyze and synthesize knowledge captured, as assigned, and share learnings.<br>• Build and refresh content knowledge and subject matter expertise. | • Transfer "new" knowledge into the knowledge repositories on the intranet and website, as assigned. |

Closely aligned with knowledge management is change management. There are two schools of thought regarding an organization's culture and knowledge management. One school feels that an organization's culture should be changed first before introducing knowledge management. The second school says to accept the organizational culture as is, and then introduce knowledge management strategies that fit the given organizational culture. Since macro-organizational cultures of large, entrenched organizations (such as the federal government) can take anywhere from ten to fourteen years to change, as Marilyn Parker points out in her book *Strategic Transformation and Information Technology* (Prentice Hall, 1996), it may be better to take the existing culture as is and then apply knowledge management and change management techniques that would match that given culture (or subculture). The thought here is that by changing some individual behaviors (e.g., through the introduction of knowledge management practices), then over time, the organizational behaviors and culture would eventually change.

According to the Business Process Reengineering Learning Center (http://www.prosci.com/chg9.htm), a study of 254 companies looked at best practices in change management. The general findings were:

- The number one contributor of top management is the ability to define and communicate the vision.
- Most companies find dealing with resistance the most difficult part of the project.
- Many change agents find that their biggest obstacles are the same people who initiated the change in the first place.
- A major reason companies use consultants from outside their organization is to avoid political agendas and biases from within their own company.

Resistance to change is a "given" in most organizations, although some people believe that it is the *fear* of resistance to change that is commonplace in organizations. In looking at human capital strategies, certain processes will undoubtedly change in order to be in better alignment with the organization's strategic mission and vision. As new processes are introduced, change management must be part of the implementation strategy—in fact, if one wants to wait and do change management towards the end of the process, then the processes won't be accepted by the users and will generally fail. The users (i.e., those individuals who will be affected by the processes) should be involved in all phases of design, development, and implementation (from the requirements generation through implementation and maintenance). In the information systems field, many systems have failed due to the "parachute philosophy" of "throwing the system over the wall and hoping that the users catch it." Change management practices need to be discussed and applied during the entire life-cycle process. Otherwise, the human capital strategy and "new processes" might be a "technical success," but a "technology transfer failure."

Let's take a case in point: NASA is introducing throughout the Agency the Integrated Financial Management Program (IFMP), which is one of its highest priority projects. According to the main website for IFMP (http://ifmp.nasa.gov), "The mission of IFMP is to improve the financial, physical, and human resources management processes throughout the Agency. IFMP, under the auspices of the Office of Chief Financial Officer, is reengineering NASA's business infrastructure and implementing enabling technology to provide better management information for decision-making." Change management has been recognized as a critical component of making IFMP successful. According to NASA (http://imfp.nasa.gov):

> *IFMP change management is the process of aligning NASA's people and culture with the impending changes in the Agency's business strategy, organizational structure, and systems. Such changes will inevitably affect the daily lives of NASA employees and managers, compelling them to change the way they do their jobs, and how they regard their roles. IFMP change management efforts will help NASA's people understand why change is happening, how change will affect their daily lives, and what they must do to succeed in the new IFMP environment. Failure to include change management in a program the size of IFMP is a major risk to program success; even the best and newest software will not help an organization if nobody wants it or understands how to use it.*

## TO SUMMARIZE . . .

This chapter discussed the importance of the four pillars that should underpin an organization's human capital strategy: competency management, performance management, knowledge management, and change management. In the following chapters, we will take a closer look at each of these areas.

# FIVE

# Knowledge Management: The Key Pillar in a Human Capital Strategy

People are the key strategic asset in an organization. According to Chris Mihm, Director of Strategic Issues at the General Accounting Office (GAO), *people policies* must be at the heart of mergers and acquisitions to achieve success. In Mihm's talk "Going Beyond Green: Strategic Transformation through Human Capital Planning" (November 14, 2002, Washington, D.C.), Mihm indicated that 80 percent of the GAO's budget goes towards people, namely salaries and earnings. Individual transformation needs to be made before organizational transformation can be achieved. Mihm outlined some key practices for organizational transformation:

- Ensure that top leadership drives the transformation.
- Establish a coherent mission and integrated strategic goals to guide the transformation.
- Focus on a key set of principles and priorities at the outset of the transformation.
- Set implementation goals and a timeline to build momentum and show progress from day one.
- Dedicate an implementation team to manage the transformation.
- Use the performance management system to help define responsibility and assure accountability for change.

- Establish a communications strategy to create shared expectations and report related progress.
- Involve employees and obtain their ideas and gain their ownership for the transformation.
- Build a world-class organization.

At the same Strategic Human Capital Planning conference on November 14, 2002, Lisa Fairhall (Branch Chief for the Personnel Policy Branch at the Office of Management and Budget, or OMB) presented a "top 10 list for getting to green" for an agency's strategic management of human capital:

1. Meet with OMB and OPM (Office of Personnel Management) to find out what they think you need to do.
2. Complete (or continue to refine) your comprehensive workforce and skills analysis and discuss outstanding issues with OMB and OPM. Get consensus on what are your critical occupations. Identify holes in the information, and work to fill in that information.
3. Identify current and projected skills gaps; understand their relationship to your ability to meet program performance goals.
4. Develop and begin to implement a strategy to address these gaps, using existing personnel flexibilities wherever possible. Focus on critical occupations.
5. Target excess organizational layers (vertical) or redundant operations (horizontal) to eliminate unwarranted duplication and layers that do not provide value added.
6. Redirect supervisory positions to line functions to better meet customer needs.
7. Show how resources are associated with human capital strategies, and how these strategies are in turn linked to specific program outcomes or improvements.

8. Address the human capital needs of competitive sourcing, e-gov, and financial management initiatives.
9. Have strategies in place to reward high performers and to address poor performance.
10. Meet again with OMB and OPM to find out what they think you need to do.

People issues are at the crux of any organizational transformation. According to Michael Munoz, Deputy Assistant Secretary of Education-Performance Improvement, the U.S. Department of Education has had 104 reorganizations, in some form or another, in ten years (Strategic Human Capital Planning Conference, Washington, D.C., November 14, 2002). Human capital needs to be integrated within the business case of the organization, as is now being done at the Department of Education. To produce a results-oriented culture, a GAO study (GAO Report-02-966) found that successful organizations understand that they must often change their culture to successfully transform themselves, and such change starts with top leadership. Thus, all evidence seems to point to the "people issues" as being the heart and soul of organizational transformation.

If people form the "body" of an organization, then their knowledge is the blood that keeps the organization alive. As a result, management of that knowledge ("knowledge management") must be a central part of an organization's human capital strategy. The following sections address what knowledge management is, and how it should play its vital role in a human capital strategy.

## Knowledge Management

A working definition of knowledge management is that it is the process of creating value from an organization's intangible assets. Simply put, knowledge management deals with how to best leverage knowledge internally and externally. Most people agree that knowledge management entails three main types of capital: human capital, structural capital, and customer capital. Human capital is primarily the brainpower of the employees. Structural capital refers to "intangibles" that can't easily be brought home with an employee, such as intellectual property rights. Customer capital, also referred to as social or relationship capital, is knowledge that is learned from the customers and fed back into the organization. All three types of capital are necessary to build "organizational intelligence" and contribute towards building a "learning organization."

Knowledge management usually has four main processes: knowledge identification and capture, knowledge sharing, knowledge application, and knowledge creation. Important knowledge in the organization is identified and captured. Then, the knowledge is shared and applied in particular situations. Finally, it becomes internalized and, it is hoped, new knowledge spawns from this application and sharing process. Knowledge management usually has three main components: process, people, and technology. *Process* refers to developing ways to embed knowledge into the daily working activities of the employees. *People* deals with how best to build and nurture a knowledge sharing culture in the organization. *Technology* deals with creating a unified knowledge network that enables the sharing of knowledge to easily take place.

## Lessons Learned from the Trenches

Why do organizations engage in knowledge management? The following list, compiled and categorized by Liebowitz, provides the various critical success factors that organizations strive to achieve in implementing their knowledge management initiatives:

**Adaptability/Agility**

- Anticipate potential market opportunities for new products/services
- Rapidly commercialize new innovations
- Adapt quickly to unanticipated changes
- Anticipate surprises and crises

- Quickly adapt the organization's goals and objectives to industry or market changes
- Decrease market response times
- Be responsive to new market demands
- Learn, decide, and adapt faster than the competition

**Creativity**

- Innovate new products or services
- Identify new business opportunities
- Learn not to reinvent the wheel
- Quickly access and build on experience and ideas to fuel innovation

**Institutional Memory Building**

- Attract and retain employees
- Retain expertise of personnel
- Capture and share best practices

***Internal* Organizational Effectiveness**

- Coordinate the development efforts of different units
- Increase the sense of belonging and community among employees in the organization
- Avoid overlapping development of corporate initiatives
- Streamline the organization's internal processes
- Reduce redundancy of information and knowledge
- Improve profits, grow revenues
- Shorten product development cycles
- Provide training, corporate learning
- Accelerate the transfer and use of existing know-how
- Improve communication and coordination across company units (i.e., reduce stovepiping)

***External* Organizational Effectiveness**

- Reach for new information about the industry and market
- Increase customer satisfaction
- Support e-business initiatives

- Manage customer relationships
- Deliver competitive intelligence
- Enhance supply chain management
- Improve strategic alliances

According to the "State of Knowledge Management" survey (*Knowledge Management Magazine*, May 2001) of 566 respondents, the following results were compiled (note: only *the top 3 responses* in each category are shown):

| *CATEGORY* | *TOP THREE RESPONSES* |
|---|---|
| Reasons for Adopting KM | 1. Retain expertise of personnel (51.9%)<br>2. Increase customer satisfaction (43.1%)<br>3. Improve profits, grow revenues (37.5%) |
| Business Uses of KM Initiative | 1. Capture and share best practices (77.7%)<br>2. Provide training, corporate learning (62.4%)<br>3. Manage customer relationships (58%) |
| Leader of the KM Initiative | 1. Crossfunctional team (29.6%)<br>2. CEO (19.4%)<br>3. CIO (12.3%)—note that the CKO was 9.0% |
| Planned Length of Project | 1. One to two years (32.4%)<br>2. Less than one year (17.3%)<br>3. Two to three years (13.6%) |
| Implementation Challenges | 1. Employees have no time for KM (41%)<br>2. Current culture does not encourage sharing (36.6%)<br>3. Lack of understanding of KM and benefits (29.5%) |
| Types of Software Purchased | 1. Messaging, e-mail (44.7%)<br>2. Knowledge base, repository (40.7%)<br>3. Document management (39.2%) |
| Spending on IT Services for KM | 1. Implementation (27.9%)<br>2. Consulting, planning (27.8%)<br>3. Training (15.3%)—Operations and outsourcing was also 15.3% |
| Software Budget Allotments | 1. Enterprise information portal (35.6%)<br>2. Document management (26.2%)<br>3. Groupware (24.4%) |

From the survey data, it appears that companies generally understand the reasons for deploying knowledge management solutions. However, the data also indicates that the implementation challenges facing knowledge management initiatives are significant and deal mostly with people and culture-oriented issues. In fact, a mantra in the knowledge management community is that KM is mostly people, culture, and process (80 to 90 percent), with technology being only 10 to 20 percent.

## CRAFTING A KNOWLEDGE MANAGEMENT STRATEGY

A knowledge management strategy framework, proposed by Chuck Seeley and William Dietrick (*KM Review*, Melcrum Publishing, 2001), can be used to develop a knowledge management strategy for an organization. There are seven components of the framework:

- *Governance:* Where should KM sit in the organization?
- *Culture:* How to create a willingness among employees to share knowledge?
- *Content Management:* What content should be included in the KM systems and processes?
- *Technology:* What technology should be used as the enabler for knowledge sharing?
- *Application:* How can the KM strategy be linked to the corporate strategy?
- *Measurement:* How to measure the value of KM?

Each of these areas will be discussed next in terms of developing an organizational knowledge management strategy.

### Governance

Governance refers to who should spearhead the KM initiatives and what kind of organizational infrastructure should be established to develop and implement the knowledge management initiatives. From the "State of Knowledge Management" survey results, a crossfunctional team was often used to lead knowledge management efforts, along with the financial and moral support (and leadership) of senior executives (the CEO, CIO, CKO, etc.). Technology, like intranets and portals, serve as an enabler for knowledge sharing, but knowledge management far exceeds implementing just a technology solution. Even though many KM efforts are led by the CIO of an organization, this may be a mistake as it may create a technology-centric approach to knowledge management. One caveat to keep in mind is that the KM crossfunctional team should be sure to have representatives from across each department, including someone from the human resources, library, and IT areas. The funding for the KM initiatives should usually come from the institutional budget for the organization.

### Culture

The culture part of the knowledge management strategy, according to Seeley and Dietrick, looks at establishing ownership, designing intuitive solutions for work processes, and changing what's important. Establishing ownership involves users in planning and development, incorporating and recognizing user contributions, and soliciting and responding to outgoing user feedback. Designing intuitive solutions for work processes involves selecting content for impact and implementing processes consistent with culture and work styles. Changing what's important refers to demonstrating value to the users, measuring use and impact, and providing the right recognition and rewards.

A knowledge audit should be conducted throughout the organization to try to identify the sources and sinks of knowledge, determine missing and available knowledge in terms of "knowledge gaps," map the interactions taking place between various organizational units or employees (this can be done by using Social Network Analysis), and determine the processes that should be used to allow the organization to be a "learning organization." The knowledge audit and knowledge mapping process will also give the users a better appreciation for how knowledge management can help them in their work, and help them feel part of the process—in effect, establishing "ownership." The knowledge audit and related cultural assessment will also help to determine the existing culture and subcultures in the organization; then knowledge management strategies can be applied that best fit that given subculture in order to achieve success and user acceptance. To provide further acceptance of KM, the knowledge management strategy should be closely aligned with the organization's overall strategic vision and mission.

A "change management" program should also be part of the organization's knowledge management strategy. As current daily work processes may be altered or enhanced as knowledge management takes a greater role in the organization, a change management program is essential so that the employees feel at ease with possible changes in their work processes.

As part of this culture shift, an organization should review its recognition and reward system to include learning and knowledge sharing proficiencies. These proficiencies would then be tied to the employee's annual performance review in order to give knowledge sharing processes greater credibility. The Human Resources Department in the organization can take the leadership role in this area, but it should involve a crossfunctional team to analyze the current recognition and reward system and make suggestions for how to improve it. Part of the resulting culture should not only celebrate successes, but also should also encourage people to openly talk about their failures and bittersweet stories. In fact, a "Significant Learning" award could be established for how lessons were shared and disseminated throughout the organization and the value-added effects of learning from these insights (whether failures or successes). In order to strive towards a "learning organization," people should feel encouraged to openly discuss their failures so that learning can take place across the organization.

## Content Management

The knowledge audit and resulting knowledge map of the organization will determine the mission, key decisions, required types of information, and best intelligence sources for a particular community. Specifically, the knowledge map will answer:

- What information exists in the organization, and where is it located?
- What expertise resides in the organization—who knows what?
- What relevant expertise resides outside the organization, where does this expertise exist, and how do I gain access to it?
- What are the best sources of relevant internal and external information?

The knowledge map will help determine what content—and what knowledge ontology or taxonomy of the content—should be part of the intranet.

Once the taxonomy and content are established, a content management process needs to be formalized to keep the content fresh, dynamic, and alive. Content managers and their roles and processes need to be developed. For example, "knowledge facilitators" should be assigned to moderate online communities. "Hot" breaking areas of knowledge should be injected within the online community and threaded discussions.

From Liebowitz's NASA experience, knowledge stewards and knowledge retention managers may be new roles for those in an organization. The knowledge stewards could be strategically placed within the various business units of the organization to develop and embed knowledge processes within the daily work activities of employees, to maintain and augment an expertise locator system within the organization, and to encourage a knowledge sharing culture. The role of knowledge retention managers may also be created to be in charge of conducting knowledge elicitation sessions with experts within the organization and external community, and of codifying and sharing lessons learned and best practices for building the institutional memory of the organization.

## Technology

From a technology viewpoint, a typical knowledge management system includes a collaboration environment, a knowledge portal, and content management tools. A collaboration environment, via the use of online communities, could be created for posting documents, having threaded discussions, and sharing insights. A knowledge portal should be created, and the employees need to be able to customize their portals for their interest areas. Content management tools (i.e., document management) such as Semio (www.semio.com), Autonomy (www.autonomy.com) and others should also be used so that content can be easily designed, developed, encoded, and maintained. The use of web-based, online searchable video for capturing video nuggets of expert interviews may be a useful technology feature within the organization's intranet and website. Streamsage (www.streamsage.com), Virage (www.virage.com), and Convera (www.convera.com) are the leading software companies producing the ability to handle online searchable video over the Web. The intranet and website should also have an efficient search engine like Google, and might need to have some visualization tools like Inxight (www.inxight.com) to better portray content within the intranet and website.

## Application

The knowledge management strategy should be a key pillar of the organization's human capital strategy, and it should be aligned with the organization's business strategy, mission, and vision. According to Seeley and Dietrick, areas of strategic importance to the organization and communities that have common objectives and/or informational needs are excellent candidates for applying knowledge management.

## Measurement

Once the knowledge management initiative is developed, a measurement approach should be constructed and applied. A standard evaluation process to measure outcomes and effectiveness metrics relating to the knowledge management initiatives should be developed. For example, Sue Hanley's work at Dell (Department of Navy *Metrics Guide for Knowledge Management Initiatives*, May 2001), indicates some possible measures for evaluating online communities and other knowledge management approaches, as shown in the following table:

| *KM Initiatives* | *System Measures* | *Outcome Measures* |
|---|---|---|
| Communities of Practice<br>• Real-time collaboration | • **Common Measures**<br>• Number of contributions<br>• Frequency of update<br>• Ratio of the number of members to the number of contributors (conversion rate)<br>• Number of members | • Savings and/or improvement in organizational quality and efficiency<br>• Captured organizational memory<br>• Reduced attrition rate for community members |
| Special Interest Group | • **Common Measures**<br>• Number of contributions<br>• Frequency of update<br>• Ratio of the number of members to the number of contributors (conversion rate)<br>• Number of members | • Savings and/or improvement in organizational quality and efficiency<br>• Captured organizational memory<br>• Reduced attrition rate for community members |
| Expertise Directory | • **Common Measures**<br>• Number of contributions<br>• Frequency of update | • Saving and/or improvement in organizational quality and efficiency |
| Lesson Learned Database<br>• Lessons about "doing the work" | • **Common Measures**<br>• Number of contributions<br>• Frequency of update | • Saving and/or improvement in organizational quality and efficiency |
| Portal | • **Common Measures**<br>• Searching precision and recall<br>• Usage of personalization features<br>• Frequency of general search versus use of predefined links<br>• Number of users with the portal as their "home page" | • Reduced time to find relevant information<br>• Reduced training time or learning curve (if portal is used to integrate multiple separate systems) |
| Collaborative Systems<br>• For design<br>• Including shared work repositories | • **Common Measures**<br>• Network reliability/quality of service<br>• Number of patents/trademarks produced<br>• Number of articles written plus number of conference presentations per employee | • Reduced cost of product development, acquisition and/or maintenance<br>• Reduction in the number of program delays<br>• Faster response to proposals<br>• Reduced learning curve for new employees |

## IMPLEMENTING A KNOWLEDGE MANAGEMENT STRATEGY AS PART OF A HUMAN CAPITAL STRATEGY

A generic knowledge management implementation framework might consist of the elements represented in Figure 5.1.

In this implementation framework, the users have certain intentions or needs for deciding to use the knowledge management system. Solutions are then provided for meeting these needs or requirements. Important factors that contribute to the solutions include: the

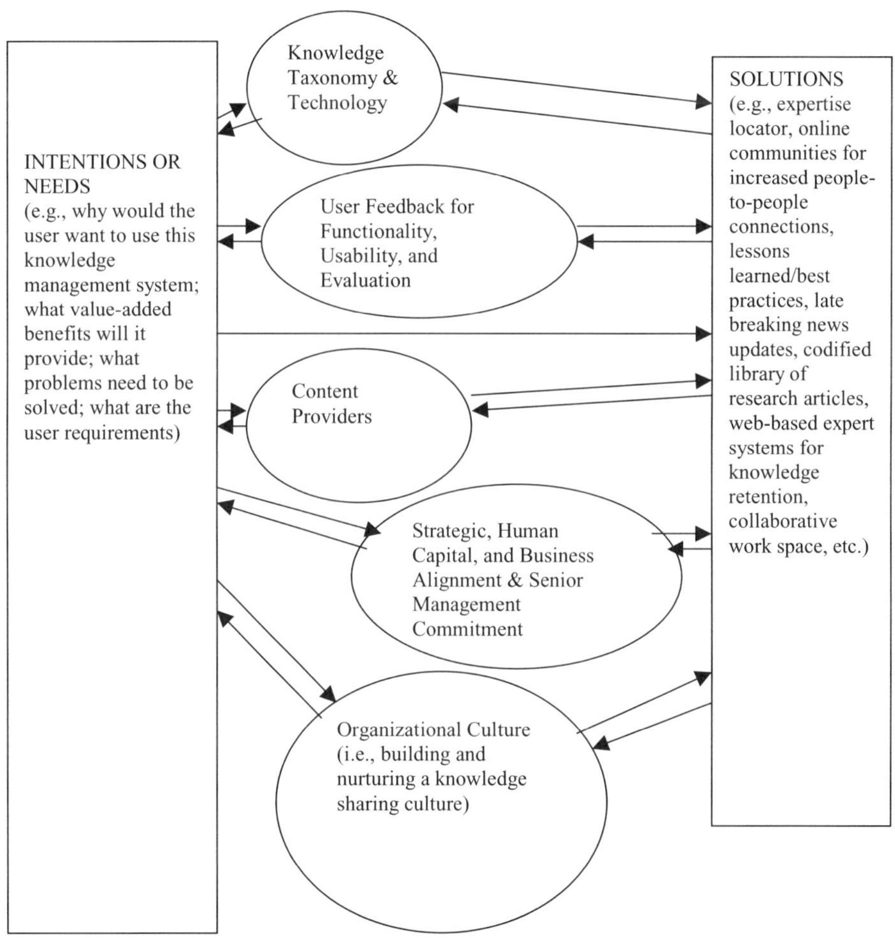


FIGURE 5.1 *A Knowledge Management Implementation Framework.*

organizational culture and how the knowledge management system affects it; the alignment of the knowledge management system with the strategic, human capital, and business goals of the organization; senior management commitment and involvement in the knowledge management system and related knowledge management efforts; user feedback on functionality, usability, and evaluation of the knowledge management system; content providers' input for codifying material as part of the knowledge management system; the knowledge taxonomy for organizing content in the knowledge management system; and technologies applied in the development and use of the knowledge management system. There is a double-loop learning process involving these factors between the intentions and solutions because each factor iteratively influences a refinement of either the intentions or the solutions. For example, an initial knowledge taxonomy is built to tag and group the content in the knowledge management system, as well as to be used as an ontology for classifying the expertise in the expert locator system. This knowledge taxonomy may be increased as new concepts are introduced and discussed in the online community part of the system or via new articles in the knowledge library that describe these emerging concepts. Thus, the knowledge taxonomy is enhanced by the two-way interactions between the users (intentions) and possible solutions.

The knowledge management processes should dovetail nicely with an organization's human capital strategy. Knowledge identification and capture processes will help identify critical "at risk" knowledge areas in the organization where "knowledge gaps" may result from soon-to-be-retired experts, and will then capture their expertise in codified and personalized ways. For example, NASA's Lessons Learned Information System (http://llis.nasa.gov) captures over 1,300 lessons learned across the various NASA Centers. This knowledge repository includes both successful and bittersweet lessons, and has a user-profiling capability whereby appropriate lessons that match a user's profile will be sent to the user as a new lesson appears. A web-based, online searchable video of "knowledge nuggets" from individuals in the organization can also be created. Work at NASA Goddard Space Flight Center involves developing a knowledge preservation project, similar to the one at Sandia National Labs, to capture project management and systems engineering expertise from Goddard experts. Besides these codified approaches, a personalization approach could also be used to have knowledge sharing forums whereby experienced project managers discuss their stories and situations with less experienced project managers (see the Knowledge Sharing Initiative at NASA—http://appl.nasa.gov). Mentoring programs, creative learning/leadership groups (as are being done at NASA Goddard and the Environmental Protection Agency—a holistic approach to engage people in "different kinds of discussions"), knowledge fairs, and the like will also help promote a greater sense of community and belonging in the organization, and help to nurture and share knowledge.

Knowledge sharing and application processes will allow the socialization and internalization effects to take place, as Professor Nonaka from University of California-Berkeley advocates. As socialization occurs, knowledge is transferred and applied to fit that individual's new perception. As the knowledge is internalized by the individual and combined with other knowledge and worldviews that the individual possesses, the hope is that new knowledge will be created (i.e., the knowledge creation step). This could lead to increased innovations, new products or services, improved customer satisfaction, and other benefits. Thus, knowledge management appears to be an excellent mechanism for building the institutional memory of the organization and helping the organization be transformed into a "learning or knowledge organization." This is where the impact of knowledge management will be felt when developing an organization's human capital strategy.

# SIX

# Pillar Two: Performance Management through a Knowledge Management Lens

One of the key four pillars of a human capital strategic plan is knowledge management, as discussed in the last chapter. The second pillar of a human capital strategy is performance management. As expressed in GAO's reports, performance management systems help create a results-oriented culture. In the September 2002 GAO Report (GAO-02-966) entitled, "Results-Oriented Cultures: Using Balanced Expectations to Manage Senior Executive Performance," several key points were highlighted:

- More progress is needed to link executive expectations for performance to organizational goals.
- Greater emphasis should be placed in fostering the collaboration within and across organizational boundaries to achieve results.
- Senior executive performance expectations to lead and facilitate change could be a critical element as agencies transform themselves.
- Selected initial implementation approaches for balancing expectations include providing useful data, requiring follow-up action, and making meaningful distinctions in performance.

In order to gain insights for U.S. agencies from other countries' performance management initiatives, GAO's report (GAO-02-862) in August 2002 looked at performance management systems of governments in Australia, Canada, New Zealand, and the United Kingdom. GAO found that these countries were creating a "line of sight" between individual and organizational goals; using competencies to provide a fuller assessment of individual performance; linking pay to individual and overall organizational performance; and fostering organizationwide commitment to results-oriented performance management.

From these studies and others, it is clear that performance management plays an important role in developing a human capital strategy. According to Hamilton Beazley, chairman of the Strategic Leadership Group and lead author of the book *Continuity Management: Preserving Corporate Knowledge and Productivity When Employees Leave* (John Wiley, 2002), it is estimated that in 2010 someone will turn 65 every seven seconds. Beazley believes that preserving knowledge continuity between incumbent and successor employees creates the requisite balance. In Anita Bruzzese's article, "Retaining Job Knowledge after Employees Exit Helps Workplace" (*Wisconsin Rapids Daily Tribune*, November 25, 2002), Beazley is interviewed and states that the key is preserving and continuing the network of relationships. Preserving, enhancing, and increasing the network of relationships is the very core of what knowledge management can offer. Knowledge management helps to connect people to people, and to connect people to critical organizational knowledge.

Fortunately, there is some hope in terms of interest in pursuing a job in the public sector. According to the 2002 graduates of Harvard's Kennedy School of Government, more than eight out of ten new public policy graduates are now working in the public sector, either in government or at nongovernmental organizations (*The Chronicle of Higher Education*, November 29, 2002). This is an increase of 35 percent from a year ago. In 2000, 58 percent of Harvard's Kennedy School graduates with master's degrees in public policy took posts in the public sector; in 2001, the proportion was 61 percent. In 2002, it was 83 percent (*The Chronicle of Higher Education*, November 29, 2002). Perhaps, some of this interest stems from increased American loyalty after the September 11 tragedy and from the increased interest in Homeland Security.

Let's review a few notions about how knowledge management can assist human capital management, and then we can see how knowledge management processes can add value to the performance management pillar of a human capital strategy. David Walker (Comptroller General of the U.S.), in his April 12, 2001, talk "Connecting People to Information," stated that knowledge management can assist human capital management in the following ways:

- It supports matrix management (i.e., with mechanisms to bring the right people with the right skills together to maximize the value and manage risk involved with any undertaking).
- It aids coordination across borders, sectors, agencies, levels, and boundaries.
- It helps leaders and employees embrace needed cultural transformations.
- It helps leaders manage change.
- It helps managers plan their IT efforts to support employees' knowledge sharing needs.
- It helps employees identify their efforts for their organization's strategic plan by assisting in building expertise, enhancing professional development, improving recruitment, and improving retention.

Certainly, bringing the right mix of people to form teams, promoting increased coordination among functional silos, and aiding leaders and employees in organizational transformation are important attributes of how knowledge management affects performance management in positive ways.

The Office of Personnel Management's "Handbook for Measuring Employee Performance" (PMD-013, September 2001), describes performance management as the systematic process of:

- **Planning** work and setting expectations
- Continually **monitoring** performance
- **Developing** the capacity to perform
- Periodically **rating** performance in a summary fashion, and
- **Rewarding** good performance.

In the next section, we take a look at how knowledge management processes can enhance these performance management processes.

## ENHANCING PERFORMANCE MANAGEMENT THROUGH KNOWLEDGE MANAGEMENT

The following table looks at both the major performance management processes and knowledge management processes:

| *Performance Management Processes* |
|---|
| Planning<br>• Set goals and measures<br>• Establish and communicate elements and standards |
| Monitoring<br>• Measure performance<br>• Provide feedback<br>• Conduct progress review |
| Developing<br>• Address poor performance<br>• Improve good performance |
| Rating<br>• Summarize performance<br>• Assign the rating of record |
| Rewarding<br>• Recognize and reward good performance |

| *Knowledge Management Processes* |
|---|
| Knowledge Identification and Capture<br>• Identify knowledge<br>• Capture knowledge |
| Knowledge Sharing<br>• Communicate knowledge<br>• Build and nurture a knowledge sharing culture |
| Knowledge Application<br>• Incorporate knowledge<br>• Reuse knowledge |
| Knowledge Creation<br>• Create knowledge |

Knowledge management and performance management are intertwined. In *An Intelligent Organization: Integrating Performance, Competence, and Knowledge Management* (John Wiley, 2002), written by the Nokia's former director of human resources, Pentti Sydanmaanlakka, key objectives for an organization include the continuous improvement of performance and competence, and the continuous application of new knowledge. In Larry Pederson's book, *Performance-Oriented Management: A Guide for Government Agencies* (Management Concepts, Inc., 2002), the importance of making a smooth transition from a management philosophy that is reactive and task-oriented to one based on a vision of accomplishment (i.e., performance improvement) is stressed. The strong linkage between performance management and knowledge management is further evidenced by Ernie Chen, a corporate knowledge strategist at JT Frank Management Center, who discusses knowledge management as the key to sustainable performance. Chen states that strategic knowledge management is about creating an innovative culture supported by collaborative technologies to secure competitive advantage and sustainable performance and to enhance productivity by leveraging on knowledge (http://www.kwx.com.my/kwx/asp/articles02/articles_0206.asp). Chen indicates that knowledge professionals are open-minded performance-oriented professionals that have the passion to develop the eight most innovative skills for tomorrow's knowledge economy: strategic thinking, knowledge responsibility, performance-directed learning, contribution in innovative teams, professional discipline, self-driven innovation habits, solution focused mindset, and personal knowledge creation.

It thus becomes clearer that knowledge management and performance management coexist and are integral parts of each other. As we delve deeper into the specific knowledge management and performance management processes previously mentioned, a number of parallels appears among these processes. First, a closed-loop system exists for both performance management and knowledge management life cycles. In the performance management life cycle, planning is initiated that leads directly to monitoring, developing, rating, and rewarding, and then back to planning. First, goals, measures, and standards are established. Then, the performance is measured, which leads to addressing poor and good performance ("developing"). Summarizing the performance is then conducted ("rating"), and recognition and rewards are given for good performance ("rewarding"), which then leads into reviewing next year's goals, measures, and standards ("planning"), and the cycle continues.

Knowledge management also has a closed-loop system whereby knowledge is identified and captured, then shared with others. Once shared, the knowledge is applied, combined with other knowledge, and internalized by individuals, who then may create new knowledge. This new knowledge then needs to be captured, shared, applied, and the cycle continues.

A second parallel between performance management and knowledge management is that recognition and reward are important factors to help motivate certain desired behaviors. An annual performance plan provides the employee with the blueprint of what goals and activities are important for the employee to accomplish in a given year. If performance on these activities is done well, the employee is typically recognized and rewarded in some way. In a similar manner, extrinsic and intrinsic rewards are important for building a knowledge sharing culture. Intrinsic rewards may relate to self-satisfaction in sharing one's knowledge with others to see them learn. In academia, this is sometimes referred to as "psychic income" (versus "real income") as professors gain satisfaction in seeing their students learn. Extrinsic rewards are also used in knowledge management, but "name recognition" appears to be one of the most important ways to recognize and reward an individual or team. For example, if Jay Liebowitz's lesson in the organization's lessons-learned information system is the most accessed and frequently used lesson by others in the organization in a given month, Jay Liebowitz may be recognized by the organization in some way. Or if Jay Liebowitz is serving as the facilitator of an online community that is achieving tremendous growth and value-added benefits in the organization, he may be recognized or rewarded in some manner. From various studies, including McClure-Wasko's work at the University of Maryland, intrinsic rewards have a greater impact in knowledge management than extrinsic rewards; however, most organizations will use a combination of both.

A third parallel between performance management and knowledge management is that time spent up front in the stages of "planning" (the first step in performance management) and "knowledge identification" (the first step in knowledge management) will produce maximum benefits later in the life cycle. Setting proper goals and measures and establishing standards, as well as agreeing and communicating these elements to the employee, are critical first steps in achieving high performance. In the same manner, critical "at risk" knowledge areas need to be identified to see where knowledge gaps may result (due to experts leaving the organization with no backup) in the organization. These areas may then be identified as prime candidates for knowledge capture activities. A knowledge audit is typically conducted whereby areas are identified in which knowledge is missing or available, where expertise may be found, and the like. A knowledge map is then created to show where the pockets of expertise exist, and what are the links and relationships between individuals or departments in an organization. Social network analysis is often used to depict communication patterns and relationships between

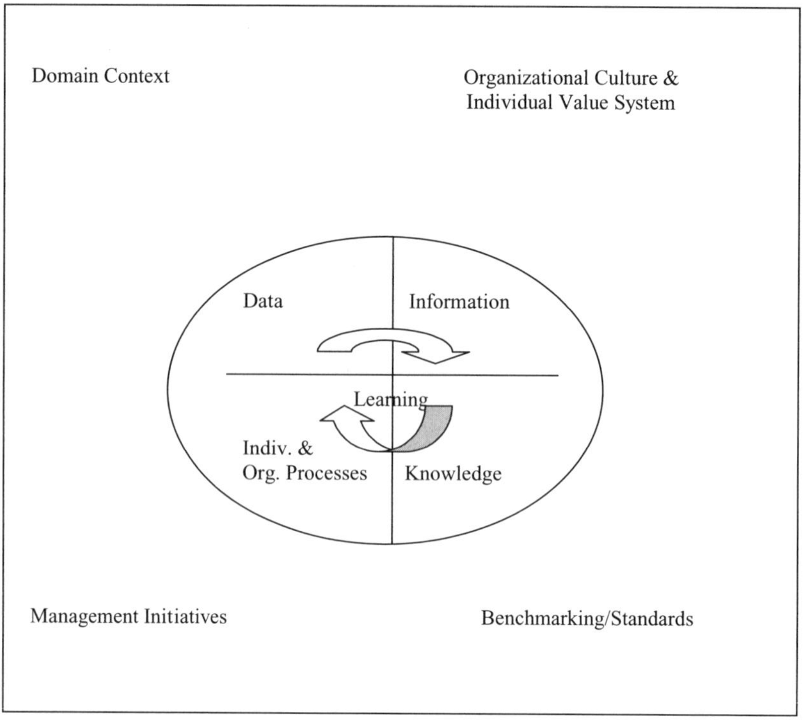


FIGURE 6.1 *Conceptual View of the Knowledge Framework.*

individuals or units in an organization. In both performance management and knowledge management, time well spent in the initial steps or processes should bear fruit in later stages of the life cycle. In the software programming milieu, if time isn't properly spent in the requirements stage, then this neglect usually leads to disaster in the encoding and testing stages.

A final parallel between performance management and knowledge management is that each area is built around a framework. In performance management, goal-setting theory is often used as a framework whereby it is hoped that good things will come to people who meet their intended goals. In knowledge management, a knowledge framework, as proposed in Figure 6.1, should first be developed in order to better understand how to share and manage knowledge.

In Figure 6.1 key components for decision-making include data, information, knowledge, and individual and organizational processes. Data is raw or discerned elements. When these elements are patterned in a certain way, data is transformed to information. Once certain rules or heuristics are applied to this information, knowledge is then created as actionable information for producing some value-added benefit. Here, knowledge is the capability to act—making information actionable. As knowledge is created and captured, learning takes place and the knowledge is applied and embedded within individual and organizational processes. The learning effect will then create new knowledge, which will then cycle through the data-information-knowledge-process transformation and iteration.

The key enablers of this knowledge framework, as defined by Jay Liebowitz and Isaac Megbolugbe, are the domain context, organizational culture, individual value system, benchmarking/standards, and management initiatives (Liebowitz and Megbolugbe, 2003). Knowledge must be applied in context in order to benefit from how it is structured or functions in that given domain. Knowledge is affected by the organizational culture as well as an individual's value system and worldview of the organization. In order for improved performance and measurement to take place, benchmarking and standards need to be created and applied (as is the case with performance management systems). Lastly, management initiatives, such as the technological infrastructure, will affect how knowledge is created, shared, and embedded within the individual, group, organization, and inter-organization. Simply put, this knowledge framework seems to be consistent with Verna Allee's view of organizational intelligence in *The Knowledge Evolution: Expanding Organizational Intelligence* (Butterworth-Heinemann, 1997); she notes that for any system (or domain), we need to know how it is structured or functions, how it learns so it can grow or improve, and how it performs in relation to certain standards. This knowledge framework integrates the concepts of knowledge, learning, and performance together in a manner that enables us to account for organizational intelligence.

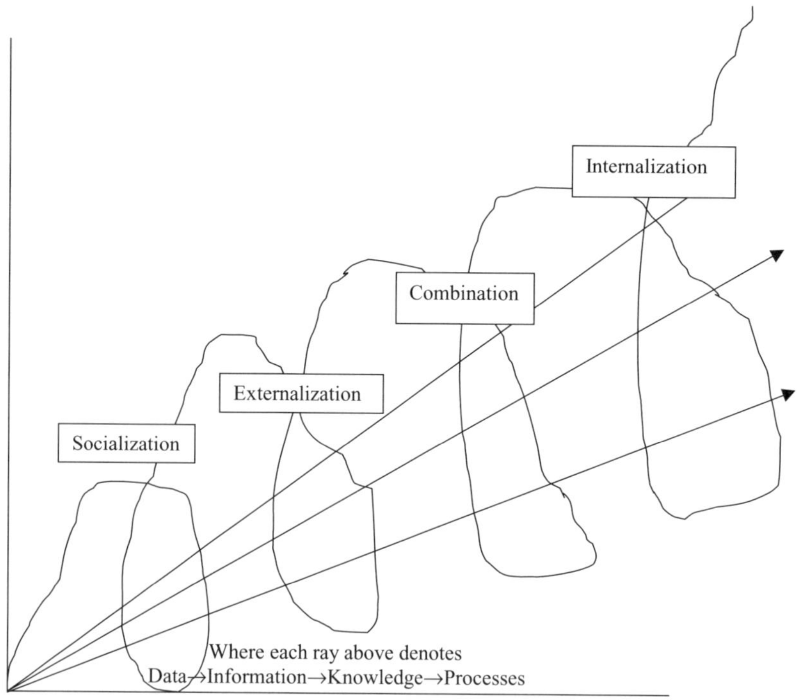


FIGURE 6.2 *The Knowledge Spiral.*

Takeuchi and Nonaka's framework for knowledge creation, as explained in their book *The Knowledge Creating Company* (Oxford University Press, 1995), can be used to connect one phase of the knowledge framework to another in a phase diagram that shows an array of planes in a trajectory extending outwards from the origin of a Cartesian graph (see Figure 6.2).

What Nonaka calls the knowledge spiral can be used as the conceptual mechanism for knowledge creation that causes the framework to move from one phase to another. The knowledge spiral (depicted above as "messy" circles due to a lack of standard transformation processes) reflects four modes of knowledge conversion that are created when tacit and explicit knowledge interact with each other. The four modes, called the "engine" of the entire knowledge creation process, are socialization, externalization, combination, and internalization. These modes, according to Takeuchi and Nonaka, are what the individual experiences; they are the mechanisms by which individual knowledge gets articulated and amplified into and throughout the organization. *Socialization* is a process of sharing experiences and creating tacit knowledge such as shared mental models. *Externalization* is a process of articulating tacit knowledge into explicit concepts (e.g., concept creation or as triggered by a dialogue). *Combination* is a process of systemizing concepts into a knowledge system, and involves combining different bodies of explicit knowledge. *Internalization* is a process of embodying explicit knowledge as tacit knowledge (e.g., learning by doing). As one moves through the knowledge levels of an individual, group, organization, and interorganization, these four modes are typically applied.

Nonaka's model is temporal, and Liebowitz-Megbolugbe's conceptual knowledge framework previously discussed is cross-sectional. By combining both Nonaka's and Liebowitz-Megbolugbe's models, the result is an integrated framework with a longitudinal view of a knowledge framework that is able to conceptually account for both creation and management of knowledge. An analogy is to view the knowledge framework as a globe. The globe can be shown to rotate on its axis. But the earth also revolves around the sun. This is the Nonaka model. When we integrate both perspectives at the same time, we are able to understand seasons. Seasons represent a metaphor for what may be called stable equilibrium.

## How Knowledge Management May Improve Performance Management

People generally prefer a strong sense of community and belonging. This bonding should ultimately improve employee morale and lead to improved performance and productivity in an organization. One of the main applications of knowledge management is online communities of practice. A typical online community allows the sharing of ideas and provides a mechanism to reach out to others for advice. The World Bank, Best Buy, Hallmark, the Federal Aviation Administration, the Defense Acquisition University (Project Management online community), NASA, and other organizations are using online communities and gaining value-added benefits. A typical online community will have a threaded discussion section, an area to post documents and announcements, and an ability to poll community members. The welcome screen of the NASA Goddard Knowledge Management online community, via the Process-Based Mission Assurance Knowledge Management System and intranets.com online community software, is shown in Figure 6.3.

Organizations may want to use online communities in order to contribute towards being a high-performing organization. For an online community to be successful, a facilitator needs to play an active role in the online community for bringing in new content, stimulating discussions, and keeping the community active and alive! Some people, such as Richard McDermott, coauthor of the book *Cultivating Communities of Practice*, feel that communities of practice are likely to become as ordinary a part of organizations as teams (http://www.onlinecommunityreport.com/features/mcdermott).

Knowledge management also helps promote people-to-people connections. Through expertise locators that serve as yellow pages of expertise in an organization, individuals can locate appropriate project team members with a complementary set of skills, find individuals in the organization with common interests, and search for individuals with certain skills needed (such as being fluent in Russian). Many companies actively use these expertise locator systems in their firms, and government agencies are trying to use them as well. However, unlike private industry, the population of these expertise locator systems in the public sector is "voluntary" due to privacy laws. NASA is trying to establish an agencywide expertise locator system through the work of the NASA Knowledge Management Team. NASA Goddard Space Flight Center has been developing their myExperts directory, as shown in Figure 6.4.

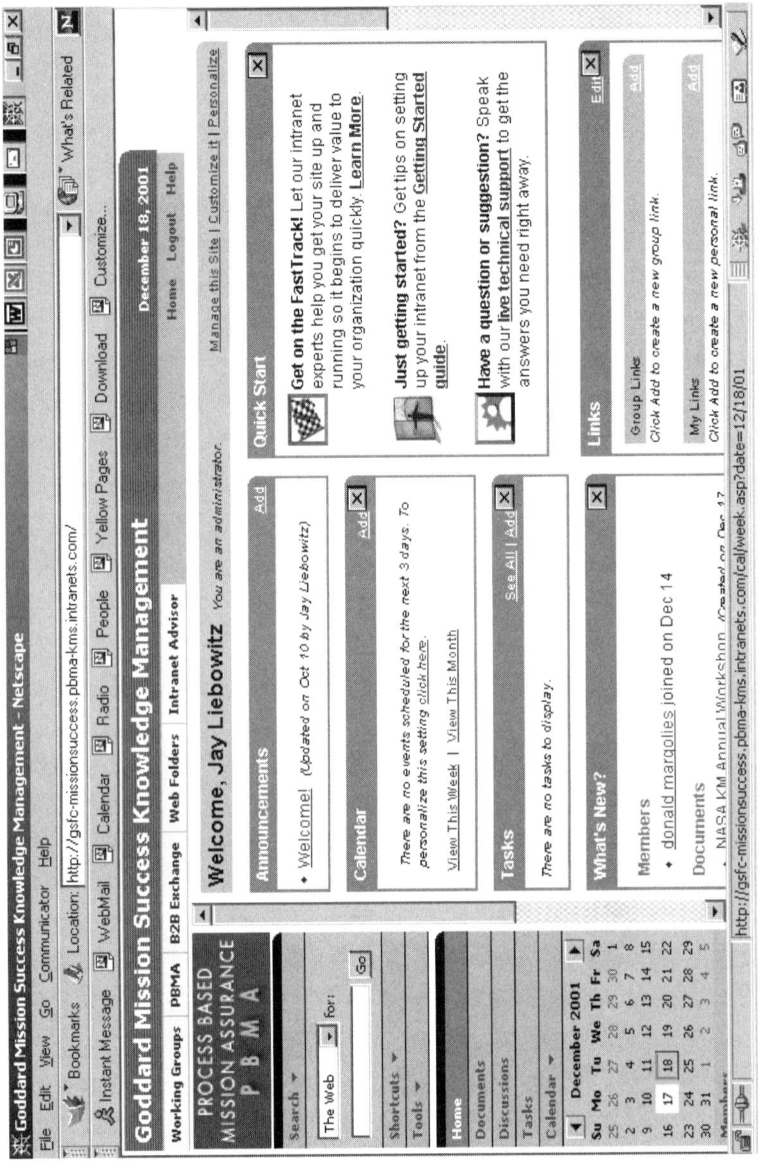


FIGURE 6.3 *Welcome Page of an Online Community.*

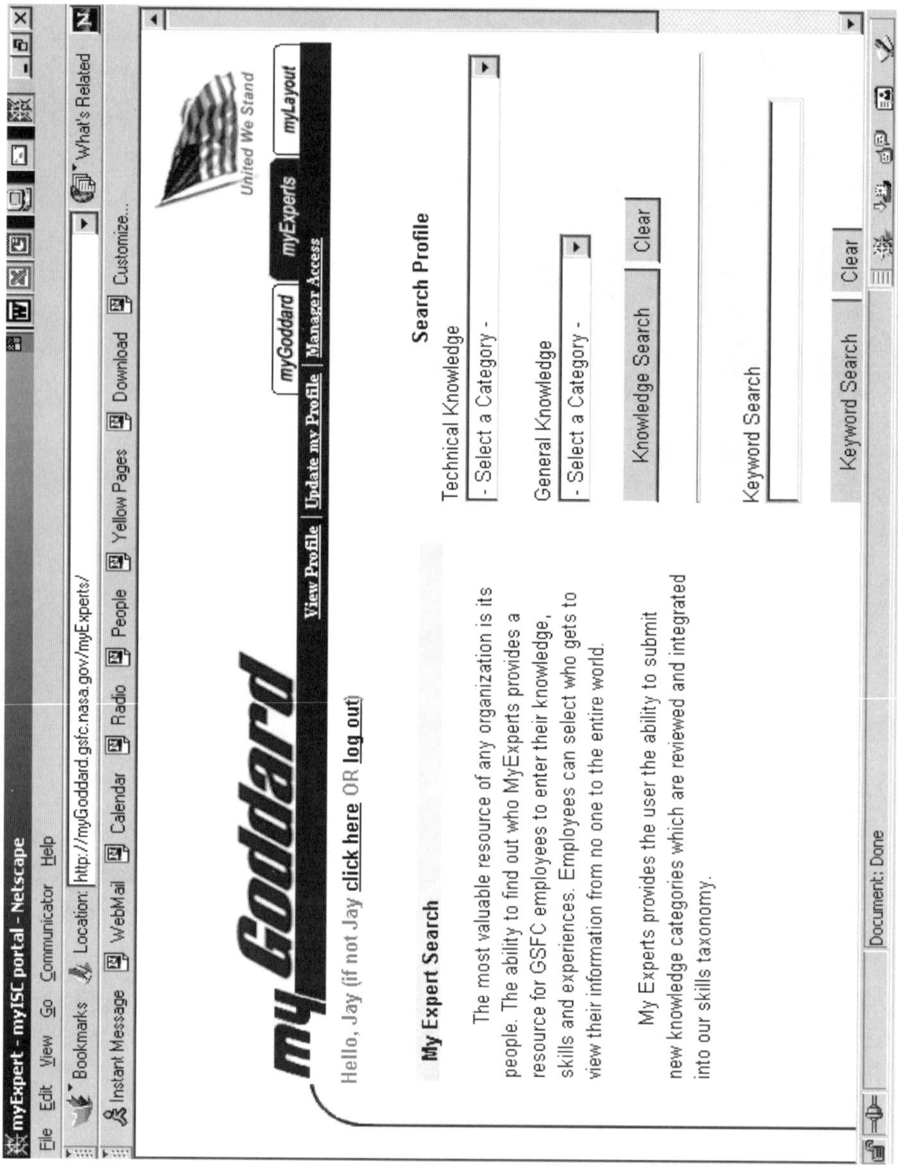


FIGURE 6.4 *MyExperts Expertise Locator.*

The hope is that by increasing people connections and the ability to go quickly to someone who may have the necessary knowledge that you need to answer your questions, then employee productivity and performance should also be enhanced. Again, the synergies between knowledge management and performance management are very apparent.

Under the "developing" stage of performance management, OPM's *Handbook for Measuring Employee Performance* indicates that providing employees with training and developmental opportunities encourages good performance, strengthens job-related skills and competencies, and helps employees keep up with changes in the workplace. Knowledge management, through the use of knowledge sharing forums and creative learning groups, allows for the personalization and transfer of knowledge to take place. Creative learning groups are being used at NASA Goddard Space Flight Center and the U.S. Environmental Protection Agency (the EPA groups are called "creative leadership groups") as a holistic approach to developing the individual, which will then help to transform the organization. Ultimately, these techniques should help in encouraging good performance.

Knowledge management also plays a role in competency and change management, the other two pillars of a human capital strategy. These areas will be discussed in the next two chapters.

# SEVEN

# Competency Management: A Necessary Pillar in a Human Capital Strategy

Competency management deals with determining the types and levels of capabilities (i.e., competencies) that an organization would like each employee to achieve in an organization. Performance management is complementary to competency management in that performance management determines how well the individual is achieving the stated competencies.

Most organizations include roles and competencies for its workforce. Roles are usually defined in the context of positions in the organization, with an attempt to fit all employees under several broad areas. There are also professional skill competencies that are common throughout the organization. For example, the U.S. Department of Transportation's Federal Highway Administration (FHWA) has a professional skills competency framework. According to this framework, there are fourteen FHWA roles: office support, administrative specialist, human resource specialist, project managers, program managers, technical managers, technical/information technology specialist, regulatory specialist, legal counsel, marketing/communications specialist, research and development specialist, team leaders, unit leaders, and senior leaders. FHWA also has categorized its competencies into two major areas, professional competencies and business management competencies, and has further developed these categories into subcategories as follows:

- **Business Management Competencies:** include competencies related to common organizational management practices and techniques.
    - *Organizational Competencies:* include planning, evaluation, and understanding the parameters in which the organization operates as well as the factors that impact the organization.
    - *Management:* represents competencies that deal with daily operations and support of the organization.
    - *Marketing:* represents competencies needed to assess customer needs and then accommodate those needs in the products and services that are subsequently offered.
- **Professional Competencies:** represent basic interpersonal competencies required to perform a job in any discipline.
    - *Communications:* represents competencies that deal with concise and effective interactions between other individuals as well as internal and external organizations.
    - *Self/Life Management:* includes balancing personal and professional characteristics appropriately to meet the demands of the workplace.
    - *Interpersonal Competencies:* deal with the quality, scope, and savvy involved in individual and group dealings.
    - *Leadership Competencies:* involve providing direction and guidance to others as well as facilitating structure and teamwork.

Then, each of these competencies are delineated further. Communications, for example, includes listening, presentation–formal, oral communication, written communication, facilitation, and media interaction. For each of the roles identified, there are three levels of proficiency that each role requires relative to each of the individual competencies. These include: Basic (must have knowledge of general terms, concepts, processes, and objectives of the competency); Intermediate (must apply the competency to perform common tasks);

and Accomplished (must use the competency to perform complex tasks requiring creativity and judgment).

Other competency frameworks and models have been developed by government agencies and the private sector. The National Academy of Public Administration (NAPA) has developed a competency model for HR (human resources) professionals that includes five components, as the following table shows (http://www.opm.gov/studies/transapp.pdf):

| *Roles* | *Competencies* |
|---|---|
| Business | • Mission oriented<br>• Strategic planner<br>• Systems innovator<br>• Understands team behavior |
| Leader | • Takes risk<br>• Ethical<br>• Decisive<br>• Develops staff<br>• Creates trust |
| HR Expert | • Knows HR principles<br>• Customer oriented<br>• Applies business procedures<br>• Manages resources<br>• Uses HR tools |
| Advocate | • Values diversity<br>• Resolves conflict<br>• Communicates well<br>• Respects others |
| Change Agent | • Manages change<br>• Consults<br>• Analyzes<br>• Uses coalition skills<br>• Influences others |

The Office of Personnel Management (OPM) Personnel Resources and Development Center has also developed a Human Resources competency model based on this model and others. The roles and competencies in the OPM Human Resources Competency Model are shown in the following table (http://www.opm.gov/studies/transapp.pdf):

| *Roles* | *Competencies* |
| --- | --- |
| Strategic Partner | • Organizational awareness<br>• Problem solving<br>• Customer service<br>• Stress tolerance<br>• Oral communication |
| Leader | • Decision-making<br>• Planning and evaluation<br>• Conflict management<br>• Self-management<br>• Self-esteem<br>• Oral communication |
| Employee Champion | • Flexibility<br>• Teaching others<br>• Learning<br>• Interpersonal skills<br>• Oral communication |
| Technical Expert | • Technical competence<br>• Legal, government, and jurisprudence<br>• Personnel and human resources<br>• Information management<br>• Arithmetic<br>• Mathematical reasoning<br>• Customer service<br>• Writing<br>• Reading<br>• Memory<br>• Attention to detail<br>• Oral communication |
| Change Consultant | • Teamwork<br>• Reasoning<br>• Influencing/Negotiating<br>• Integrity/Honesty<br>• Creative thinking<br>• Oral communication<br>• Stress tolerance |

As another example of an HR competency framework, the Department of Defense (DoD) has developed an HR competency framework. They have various positions including human resources generalists, staffing specialists, classification specialist, labor relations specialist, employee development specialist, personnel systems manager, personnel support, and DoD manager. The competencies are (http://www.opm.gov/studies/transapp.pdf) shown in the following table:

| | |
|---|---|
| Business Management Competencies | • Business process reengineering<br>• Change management<br>• Contract management<br>• Cost-benefit analysis<br>• Customer relations<br>• Financial management<br>• Marketing<br>• Negotiating<br>• Organizational awareness<br>• Organizational needs assessment<br>• Outcome measures and evaluation<br>• Project management<br>• Strategic human resource practices<br>• Strategic planning |
| Professional Competencies | • Coaching and mentoring<br>• Communication<br>• Conflict management<br>• Decision-making<br>• Ethics<br>• Facilitation<br>• Interpersonal relations<br>• Problem-solving<br>• Self-management<br>• Teamwork<br>• Technology application |
| Technical HR Competencies | • Appeals, grievances, and litigation<br>• Attendance and leave<br>• Benefits |

- Career development
- Compensation
- Discipline and adverse action
- Employee assistance
- Equal employment opportunity
- Human resource management fundamentals
- Instructional systems development
- Instructional technology
- Job analysis
- Labor management relations
- Organizational development
- Organization and position design
- Pay administration
- Performance management
- Personnel assessment
- Personnel systems management
- Position classification
- Reduction-in-force
- Rewards and recognition
- Staffing and recruiting
- Succession planning

---

The State Government of Maine has a Final Management Competency Model that includes leadership competencies, effective problem-solver competencies, and stewardship competencies. Under leadership competencies, the following apply: models integrity, effective communicator, supportive coach, and visionary. For effective problem-solver competencies, one should be an analytical thinker, a systems thinker, and creative. For stewardship competencies, the following apply: being customer-focused and results-oriented, and having sound judgment (http://www.state.me.us/bhr/mms/Final%20Competency%20Model.htm).

In the United Kingdom, the Government Information and Communication Service has developed a competency framework. Eight competencies are highlighted in this framework (http://www.gics.gov.uk/downloads/competence-framework-final.pdf):

- *Professional knowledge:* you develop and apply your communications expertise to achieve results and improve professional practice.
- *Determination:* you overcome obstacles and maximize your impact and personal contribution.
- *Creativity:* you offer creative and imaginative ways to better communicate and solve problems.
- *Communication:* you ensure that your message is clear and that it is understood.
- *Cooperation:* you have productive working relationships within and beyond the team.
- *Judgment:* you offer well-thought-out solutions to problems and take sound decisions.
- *Organization:* you deliver projects and results on time within available resources.
- *Leadership and vision:* you inspire the team with a clear vision and sense of purpose.

The September 2001 GAO Report on "Human Capital: Practices that Empowered and Involved Employees" (GAO Report-01-1070) discusses the importance of applying approaches so that government employees feel empowered to make appropriate, well-informed decisions. The report echoes the need for many of the competencies previously cited and suggests that employee empowerment is a critical component for achieving these competencies at high levels of proficiency. The full GAO report is included at the end of the book.

## Knowledge Management and Competency Management

Knowledge management deals with the process of creating value from an organization's intellectual assets. In order to produce value, there needs to be some attributes or competencies to measure. A categorized list of possible critical success factors to determine knowledge management success in an organization, as previously discussed, is:

**Adaptability/Agility**
- Anticipate potential market opportunities for new products/services
- Rapidly commercialize new innovations
- Adapt quickly to unanticipated changes
- Anticipate surprises and crises
- Quickly adapt the organization's goals and objectives to industry/market changes
- Decrease market response times
- Be responsive to new market demands
- Learn, decide, and adapt faster than the competition

**Creativity**
- Innovate new products/services
- Identify new business opportunities
- Learn not to reinvent the wheel
- Quickly access and build on experience and ideas to fuel innovation

**Institutional Memory Building**
- Attract and retain employees
- Retain expertise of personnel
- Capture and share best practices

**Organizational *Internal* Effectiveness**
- Coordinate the development efforts of different units
- Increase the sense of belonging and community among employees in the organization
- Avoid overlapping development of corporate initiatives
- Streamline the organization's internal processes
- Reduce redundancy of information and knowledge
- Improve profits, grow revenues

- Shorten product development cycles
- Provide training, corporate learning
- Accelerate the transfer and use of existing know-how
- Improve communication and coordination across company units (i.e., reduce stovepiping)

**Organizational *External* Effectiveness**

- Reach to new information about the industry and market
- Increase customer satisfaction
- Support e-business initiatives
- Manage customer relationships
- Deliver competitive intelligence
- Enhance supply chain management
- Improve strategic alliances

The tutorial outline titled "KM Quick: A KM Tool for Government Practitioners," developed by the Federal Aviation Administration Knowledge Services Network and the Federal Knowledge Management Network (August 22, 2002, Washington, D.C.; http://www.km.gov), describes the twenty-first–century knowledge environment as one involving accelerating change, increasing uncertainty, a growing need for knowledge and learning, and exploding innovation. The knowledge imperative for the government, as discussed in the KM Quick tutorial outline, is that knowledge must be leveraged through e-government, a KM capacity throughout government must be built, learning how to learn across all government agencies and offices is needed, and applying KM to emerging challenges in government (e.g., Homeland Security) must be accomplished.

A white paper on "Skills Management in Knowledge-Intensive Organizations" (Intelligent Software Components, April 2002, http://www.isoco.com) asserts that organizations surviving in the "knowledge economy" must capitalize on the principal asset for the organization—namely, its intellectual capital. In this paper, people are viewed as sellers of knowledge, while departments, projects, profiles, and organizations are viewed as knowledge buyers. Together, they comprise a knowledge market where the goods to be traded are competencies.

This knowledge market approach is quite interesting. Other organizations have developed other types of models to look at "knowledge organizations." The company Tip Interactive (http://www.tipinteractive.com/elearningsuite/default.asp) looks at a performance improvement toolbox as an atom that has a knowledge nucleus. The electrons circling around the nucleus are competency development, performance management, knowledge management, e-learning, and employee orientation. Here, we see the importance of the pillars that we have been discussing as forming the foundation for an organization's human capital strategy.

In an earlier chapter, we discussed how the Public Service of Canada is using "competency-based management (CBM)," which combines elements of competency management and performance management. According to the "Framework for CBM in the Public Service of Canada" (http://www.tbs-sct.gc.ca/hr_connexions_rh/sigs/CBHRM/framework_cbm/fcbm1_e.html), CBM is the application of a set of competencies to the management of human resources to achieve both excellence in performance and results that are relevant to the organization's business strategies. CBM is based on the "what" and "how" of managing employee performance. Essentially, the work to be performed ("what") plus the performance of the worker ("how") equals results that should add value to the organization.

According to the Public Service of Canada's *CBM Framework*, there are certain conditions usually considered necessary for CBM to be successful. They include:

- The organization should have a culture that fosters participatory decision-making, innovation, individual flexibility, growth, excellence in performance, and continuous learning.

- All levels of management should assume a strong leadership and championship role for the long-term.
- Senior management needs to agree on a specific direction that is consistent across the organization.
- The project should have the commitment, participation, and long-term buy-in of key stakeholders.
- The culture of the organization should encourage managers to take ownership and drive the process throughout the implementation cycle.
- The organization needs to have a strong communication strategy in place to ensure that employees understand the reason for implementing CBM and how it can help contribute to results.
- Competencies need to be applied correctly—if not, they become meaningless.

Within the Public Service of Canada, competency profiles exist at various levels. The number of competencies vary across profiles, but most models tend to list between ten and thirty competencies (http://www.tbs-sct.gc.ca/hr_connexions_rh/sigs/CBHRM/framework_cbm/fcbm1_e.html). According to the Public Service of Canada, most organizations should have in place a measurement system capable of differentiating performance in terms of its efficiency and effectiveness.

As can be seen from the various competency models and frameworks described, an organization's human capital strategy needs to incorporate a competency management component. If an organization wants to build and nurture a knowledge sharing culture to maximize collaboration and synergy across the organization, various knowledge sharing competencies should also be part of the competency management model. For an organization to espouse knowledge management and become a "knowledge organization," these knowledge sharing competencies are critical to the fabric of the organization. For example, the World Bank (which wants to be known as "the

Knowledge Bank") includes learning and knowledge sharing factors as part of their annual employee performance evaluation. These factors include being open to new ideas and continuous learning; sharing one's own knowledge, learning from others, and appling knowledge in daily work; and building partnerships for learning and knowledge sharing.

A number of organizations have already created knowledge sharing as a guiding principle for the organization. For example, the Public Service Commission in Canada has "Knowledge, Information, and Data Should be Shared" as one of its four guiding principles. Specifically, they indicate:

- Sharing will be rewarded. We will create an environment where people feel free to contribute what they know and to seek out knowledge from colleagues.
- Performance evaluations should be linked to how well a person contributes to generating, assessing, and transferring knowledge.
- Knowledge will be available to all employees except where there is a demonstrated need for confidentiality or protection of privacy.
- Our knowledge will be shared to support collaboration with other federal government departments, other levels of government, and our other partners.
- We will establish processes and tools to enable us to capture and share our knowledge in order to support collaboration.

Certainly, it is clear that knowledge management, competency management, and performance management go hand-in-hand and are critical components for an organization's human capital strategy.

The other missing pillar, which will be described in the next chapter, is change management.

# EIGHT

# Change Management: The Forgotten Pillar

In developing a human capital strategy for an organization there are four key pillars that should be included: knowledge management, performance management, competency management, and change management. Change is inevitable for any organization, and learning how to cope with change is crucial for producing high-performing entities. When introducing a strategic human capital plan for an organization, change management needs to be a key component of this plan. Developing a change management program as part of the human capital strategy is not an easy task. As Dianne Waddell and Amrik Sohal of Monash University write in their article, "Resistance: A Constructive Tool for Change Management" (*Management Decision*, vol. 36, no. 8, 2001), one-half to two-thirds of all major corporate change programs fail. Waddell and Sohal feel that "resistance" is often cited as a key contributor to change failure, but they believe that resistance may be an ally to assist the change effort. They indicate that in an organizational setting, resistance is an expression of reservation that normally arises as a response to change. They point out some management implications to consider when encountering resistance (http://www.managementfirst.com/articles):

- Resistance may not be the enemy: it is much more complex than it may first appear. Make sure that you fully understand the reasons why it exists in your situation, and persevere in your attempts to get to the bottom of those reasons.

- If your workplace is marked by passivity or apathy, implementing change may be a difficult task.
- Encourage true participation in change: involve employees and allow them the opportunity to give feedback.

In developing a human capital strategy, there will invariably be changes in structures, processes, goals, activities, competencies, performance elements, and the like. Some believe that resistance to change is actually part of a seven-stage psychological adaptation sequence (http://www.managementfirst.com/articles):

1. *Discovery:* I've heard a rumor . . . is it true?
2. *Denial:* It doesn't affect me.
3. *Passive resistance:* I won't do anything to assist the change.
4. *Active resistance:* I'll actively sabotage the change.
5. *Exploration:* Let's try small steps in the new way of working.
6. *Commitment*: This is great; let's have more.
7. *Broadcast:* Let me tell you about this great new process.

According to ManagementFirst members, the key to successfully managing change is to effectively handle the transition between stages 4 and 5. Additionally, focus on the organization's mission and core competencies are important elements in successful change. One example that exhibits organizational change involves the Los Alamos National Laboratory. As the Cold War ended and the need for the development of nuclear weapons has been reduced, the mission of Los Alamos has had to change. According to Richard Ringer and Kelly Strong's article "Managerial Perceptions of Change at a National Laboratory" in *Leadership and Organization Development Journal* (vol. 19, no. 1, 1998), the guiding principle for Los Alamos' new mission was to become a customer-focused organization that builds on historical strengths in science and technology. A restructuring of the Laboratory took place, and employees wanted answers to questions such as "why are we reorganizing?" Part of the difficulty was the failure of management to take the necessary time to fully develop a shared sense of the new mission and common vision for the organization. As Ringer and Strong point out, perhaps a "form follows function" perspective should have been taken, whereby emphasis should have been put on working out the vision and mission issues and then trying to figure out how work gets done at Los Alamos. Certainly, the Human Resources Department had some significant challenges in dealing with training and development needs, implementation of new personnel policies and procedures, and addressing employee concerns and fears. Performance-based appraisals and employee empowerment brought in by the change plan were new human resources practices at Los Alamos.

Let's take a look how change management plays a role in knowledge management, and then see how knowledge management can facilitate change management in terms of developing and implementing a human capital strategy.

## Change Management in Knowledge Management and Vice Versa

For knowledge management to be successful, the organization must undergo some form of cultural change. In the same manner, developing and implementing a human capital strategy for an organization also involves change management. Bob Lewis, in his article "On-Demand Knowledge Management: A Two-Tier Architecture" in *IT Professional* (January/February 2002), refers to John Kotter's eight-step process for changing an organization's culture, as outlined in Kotter's book *Leading Change* (Harvard Business School Press, 1996):

1. Creating a sense of urgency
2. Establishing the guiding coalition
3. Developing a vision and strategy
4. Communicating the change vision
5. Empowering employees for broad-based action
6. Generating short-term wins
7. Consolidating gains and producing more change
8. Anchoring new approaches in the culture

Bob Lewis, the Director of Knowledge Management at Mitretek Systems in Virginia, feels that these steps (especially steps 1, 3, 4, 5, and 6) are important for knowledge management to be successful. He feels that the overall knowledge management plan must include a change management program that emphasizes collaboration and sharing. He further states that, traditionally, change management has been a separate initiative that precedes the knowledge management system's actual deployment. Such an approach, according to Lewis' experience, can delay deployment by more than a year. Lewis feels that the change management process should be incorporated into the knowledge management initiative so that both advance together.

Dr. Andy Macdonald, a former Comptroller General of Canada and the first Chief Information Officer for the federal governments of both Canada and Australia, feels that successful change management in the government requires a visible, senior champion, communication, and Kotter's principles, as listed above (http://www1.worldbank.org/publicsector/pe/changeman.htm). Steven Kelmen, a Harvard professor and former administrator of OMB's Office of Federal Procurement Policy, in his article "Sowing Seeds of Change" (*Government Executive Magazine*, October 1, 2000), indicates that the challenge is to find features of the existing culture, even if they're not dominant, that can serve as a basis for reforms. Kelmen also cites research showing that the best path to attitude change often starts with behavioral change. Kelmen points out that a key advantage of government organizations over the private sector is that employees in public service have a strong sense of mission. This could be used to constitute a basis for reform.

In April 2002, the first Chief Knowledge Officer (CKO) Summit for the Public Sector was held by TFPL, Inc. in Bath, England. Public sector CKOs gathered to discuss common areas of interest and the challenges they faced in knowledge management. One of the chief barriers to knowledge initiatives in the public sector was identified as "changing behaviors and culture." A key learning from the Summit was to focus on changing behavior, not culture. If behavior changes, culture change will follow. According to the Summit, within government there are some crossfunctional groups, but they tend to be independent, not connected together, and certainly not connected to policy-making. They really need to be connected.

According to the writings of Warren Bennis, Kenneth Benne, and Robert Chin, editors of *The Planning of Change* (Holt, Rinehart, and Winston, 1969,) and the change management experience of Fred Nickols (http://home.att.net/~nickols/change.htm), there are four basic change management strategies as shown in the following table:

*Change Management Strategies*

| *Strategy* | *Description* |
|---|---|
| Rational-Empirical | People are rational and will follow their self-interest, once it is revealed to them. Change is based on the communication of information and the proffering of incentives. |
| Normative-Reeducative | People are social beings and will adhere to cultural norms and values. Change is based on redefining and reinterpreting existing norms and values, and developing commitments to new ones. |

*Change Management Strategies* (continued)

| *Strategy* | *Description* |
|---|---|
| Power-Coercive | People are basically compliant and will generally do what they are told or can be made to do. Change is based on the exercise of authority and the imposition of sanctions. |
| Environmental-Adaptive | People oppose loss and disruption but they adapt readily to new circumstances. Change is based on building a new organization and gradually transferring people from the old one to the new one. |

According to Nickols, a change management expert, an organization usually applies a mix of strategies as opposed to a single change strategy. Some of the factors to consider when determining the right mix are:

- Degree of resistance
- Target population
- The stakes
- The time frame
- Expertise
- Dependency

If, for example, there is a short time frame, then a power-coercive strategy might be best.

Another important factor concerns the level of trust in the organization. For online communities to be successful, trust among the community members needs to be built and maintained. The effect of interorganizational trust on knowledge cooperation has been documented in a number of articles, including Vijay Khandelwal and Petter Gottschalk's 2003 paper titled "Information Technology Support for Interorganizational Knowledge Transfer: An Empirical Study of

Law Firms in Norway and Australia" (*Information Resources Management Journal*, vol. 16, no. 1, Idea Group Publishing, January–March 2003).

How does change management and knowledge management relate to human capital strategy? In the October 2002 issue of *HR Magazine*, the cover story by Steve Bates is "Accounting for People: HR Strives to Measure the Value of Human Capital." In the article, David Norton (one of the founders of the Balanced Scorecard) indicates that people are looking for leading indicators of a company's success, and human capital investment is one of the best. People must be thought of as an asset, not an expense. Human capital measurement, empowered teams (as used at Dow Chemical), and clear communication of strategic directions are examples of important attributes that affect achieving the mission of an organization.

Dan Caterinicchia, in his article "Cultural Change Trumps Technology" in *Federal Computer Week* (January 7, 2002), states that government experts indicate that technology is important, but the key to making knowledge management programs work is changing an agency's business culture. According to John Cabral, director of the office of knowledge management at the U.S. State Department, and Bao Nguyen, chief of the Air Force's information and knowledge management division, culture change is the key to success.

Let's now take a look at NASA, a government agency that is a strong believer in change management.

## NASA: Applying Change Management Strategies

Sean O'Keefe, in his speech "NASA Update" on December 11, 2002, talked about moving the agency towards a "One NASA" approach. According to the One NASA website (http://www.onenasa.nasa.gov), One NASA is an effort to foster greater collaboration across the Agency, and its focus is *cultural change*. Similar sets of cultural challenges face the newly formed Department of Homeland Security, comprised of 170,000 persons from twenty-two agencies.

Complementary programs to the One NASA concept, such as the Integrated Financial Management Program (IFMP) and Freedom to Manage, are promoting common business practices across NASA. Let's look at IFMP change management to get a fuller appreciation for the importance of a change management program.

## INTEGRATED FINANCIAL MANAGEMENT PROGRAM CHANGE MANAGEMENT

The mission of the IFMP is to improve the financial, physical, and human resources management processes throughout NASA, as stated in the IFMP Change Management Strategy (Office of the Chief Financial Officer, NASA, Revised July 2001; http://ifmp.nasa.gov/programoffice/changemgmt.html). Bringing online new agencywide processes, systems, practices, and structures for these activities is a challenge, and NASA has recognized the importance of applying change management techniques to make IFMP a reality. Change, as expressed in the IFMP Change Management Strategy report, refers to organizational change, both in the sense of changing the organization itself (its assets, structures, systems, etc.), and in terms of changing organizational behavior. Organizational behavior refers to the individual behavior of people in the organization and the collective behavior of the Agency.

According to the IFM Program Office website (http://ifmp.nasa.gov/programoffice/changemgmt.html), IFMP change management is the process of aligning NASA's people and culture with the impending changes in the agency's business strategy, organizational structure, and systems. IFMP is taking a two-prong approach to change management. First, consistent change management efforts at the user level are being supported. In this manner, according to the IFM Program Office, "NASA managers and staff will be ready to work with the new systems and processes, and they will understand how their jobs have changed." The second part of the IFMP change management program is focusing on facilitating change at the leadership level and helping leaders articulate how they will use IFMP to drive fundamental change in their organizations (http://ifmp.nasa.gov/programoffice/changemgmt.html).

The NASA IFMP team is looking at change management as encompassing many different activities, but it is concentrating on communications, training, and transition activities. The IFM Program Office is serving as the central change management office and a key change agent for the program. Part of the Program Office is the corporate change management team. The NASA Centers also have IFM steering committees, project implementation teams, and implementation support teams.

The Transition Strategy deals with those activities, outside of training and communications, that are necessary to align people and culture with changes to systems and processes (NASA IFMP Change Management Strategy Report). As such, these activities relate to the transformational level (strategic) and the transactional level (tactical). Activities and actions are being developed to design change activities, implement change activities, and sustain changed behavior.

The Communications Strategy is critical for delivering the program vision and strategy to all essential stakeholders. According to the IFMP Change Management Strategy Report, the IFM Program Office is incorporating a number of "industry" communications best practices, including:

- Establishing concise, attainable objectives in support of the business case
- Identifying key audiences as those who can make or break the effort
- Creating a few clear, concise, and repeatable messages
- Delivering messages via many messengers and a range of vehicles
- Creating content that shifts perceptions, spurs actions, and achieves results

- Gathering feedback on the impact and effectiveness of the communications effort
- Using feedback to refine and adjust the effort on an ongoing basis

According to the IFMP Change Management Strategy Report (http://ifmp.nasa.gov/programoffice/changemgmt.html), the Training Strategy involves the education and training of NASA staff—to perform new tasks, apply new technology, fulfill new roles, and engage in new work behaviors as related to the IFMP. The IFM Program's mission with respect to training and learning is to (http://ifmp.nasa.gov/programoffice/changemgmt.html):

- Develop and articulate a comprehensive learning strategy for IFM
- Coordinate and monitor execution of the IFM learning strategy
- Develop learning interventions to support agency-level transformation
- Support and offer guidance to implementing centers and their projects
- Establish standards and procedures for instructional methods and learning technology approaches

The change management program will greatly determine the success of the IFMP. NASA has recognized up front the importance of change management, and by applying the right change management strategies, IFMP should be successful.

## Change Management, Knowledge Management, and Human Capital

Many organizations aspire to becoming a learning, collaborative, knowledge-sharing entity. To make this a reality, organizations must invest in their people and nourish their intellectual roots. Developing a human capital strategy for an organization is people-centric, and as such a learning strategy should be part of this overall human capital strategy. NASA developed an IFM learning strategy that has employee and organization development as its keystone. The NASA Policy Directive 3410 on Employee and Organizational Development states:

> *To support the full utilization of the NASA workforce in achieving NASA's strategic outcomes, it is NASA policy to make training and development opportunities widely available to employees to enhance individual capabilities; build and retain a skilled and effective workforce; improve organization performance; and maintain scientific, professional, technical, and management proficiency.*

Replenishing the intellectual (and emotional) wealth of the employees is an integral part of building a vital human capital knowledge base and developing a learning organization. As employees learn, relearn, and unlearn various methods, practices, techniques, systems, and knowledge, they will undergo various changes in how they internalize and apply their new learning in the organization. Thus, change management becomes ever more important as individual learning is transformed into organizational knowledge.

One way to prevent a perceived threat or loss of competitive edge on the part of the workforce in the process of building a knowledge sharing culture, is by tapping into the organization's retiree community. The U.S. State Department is capturing retirees' knowledge by interviewing ambassadors and other retiring employees with questions related to the specifics of their job and then making this knowledge available online via the State Department's enterprise system. The Air Force is using exit interviews to capture the knowledge of departing personnel in order to train their replacements, according to Bao Nguyen, Chief of the Air Force's information and knowledge management division (http://www.fcw.com/fcw/articles/2002/0107/mgt—

culture-01-07-02.asp). NASA Goddard Space Flight Center has also launched a knowledge preservation project to capture key knowledge from retirees and experts in the project management and systems engineering areas. NASA has a Knowledge Sharing Initiative through its Academy for Program and Project Leadership (http://appl.nasa.gov), and has encoded several hundred video nuggets of NASA expert knowledge through its Process-Based Mission Assurance Knowledge Management System (http://pbma.hq.nasa.gov). Retirees can be wonderful contributors to an organization's human capital strategy, especially in the knowledge retention and mentoring areas. Hiring them as part-time retired annuitants, subcontractors, consultants, and through emeritus programs may be formal mechanisms to engage the services of these individuals. Many retirees are pleased to be able to "give back" to their beloved organization, so they may be willing to provide their help and insight for altruistic reasons. They have been overlooked in many human capital strategies, and utilizing their knowledge and expertise could be a real missing link.

In organizational life, change is a variable that is a part of every organization's equation for survival. Companies need to be adaptive and agile in order to handle the changing market forces. In the same manner, government agencies need to be customer-focused, results-oriented, streamlined, and less hierarchical in order to become high-performing organizations. As movement continues in this direction, changes will ultimately take place, and the human capital strategy must reflect how to cope with these changes from a humanistic view. Thus, a change management pillar should be a key foundation of an organization's human capital strategy.

# NINE

# Establishing Strategic Partnerships for Human Capital

Organizations are realizing that their human capital extends beyond their permanent full-time employees. In today's environment, organizations have expanded their reach to include other groups that are critical in achieving the mission of the organization. These entities include contractors, part-time employees, outsources, interims, temps, consultants, universities, international partners, strategic third-party suppliers, and others.

In a briefing on competitive advantage through people, the London Business School describes key ideas on managing human capital strategically (http://www.bestofbiz.com/briefings):

- People are the key strategic resource in an information-based, knowledge-intensive, service-driven economy.
- Competing for the hearts and minds of talented people and their knowledge and/or technical expertise is just as crucial as competing for markets and customers.
- Rather than just allocating financial capital to competing projects, programs, units, or divisions and leveraging them for a financial return on investment, top managers should also nurture individuals' expertise and initiative and leverage those qualities through sharing knowledge across the organization.
- Employees should be seen as more than raw material to be acquired and consumed.

- Responsibility for the strategy of developing people lies with the chief executive, the top team, and all managers.

The London Business School also found that leveraging human capital is typically done through social interaction and informal social networks. Managers should therefore nurture these networks and identify key players. For example, at British Petroleum, social networks were developed and encouraged. British Petroleum created cross-unit collaboration and knowledge sharing through online communities and "peer assists/peer groups"; for example, frontline people in one unit were encouraged to contact someone in another unit for advice on a problem or task, and business units engaged in similar activities and facing similar challenges were established (http://www.bestofbiz.com/briefings).

The strategic use of human capital can lead to increased innovation in an organization. For a 2001 white paper titled "Building and Exploiting Intellectual Capital: The Role of Social, Human and Physical Resources," Smith, Collins, and Clark of the University of Maryland–College Park did a field study of fifty-seven public high-technology firms and found that a firm's rate of innovation is a function of the level of intellectual capital in the organization. Intellectual capital, in turn, is predicted based on the level of physical, human, and social capital, and the interaction of these variables with intellectual capital. Smith and his colleagues found that the effects of intellectual capital on the level of innovation were greater when combined with high social, human, and physical capital. Smith indicated that "organizations benefit most from knowledge development capability when they hire smart, well-educated, experienced knowledge workers with strong tie networks and put them in an environment that is rich in physical resources."

David Walker, in his July 18, 2002, testimony "NASA Management Challenges: Human Capital and Other Critical Areas Need to be Addressed" to the Committee on Science, Subcommittee on Space and

Aeronautics, House of Representatives (GAO-02-945T), said that "the agency [NASA] is taking on a major transformation aimed at eliminating stovepipes, becoming more integrated and results-oriented, and reducing risks while working more economically, efficiently, and effectively." NASA has developed a strategic human capital plan and is developing an agencywide workforce planning and analysis system.

Across the federal government, one important problem facing agencies is the lack of a consistent strategic approach to marshaling, managing, and maintaining the human capital needed to maximize government performance and ensure its accountability. NASA's strategic human capital plan incorporates strategies, tactical actions, and metrics to support human capital goals. According to Walker, NASA is pursuing the following (GAO-02-945T):

- Renewed attention to hiring applicants just out of college and intentions to pursue this even more aggressively in coming years.
- Using the Federal Career Intern Program to hire recent science and engineering graduates.
- Supplementing the workforce with nonpermanent civil servants, where it makes sense.
- Implementing a program to repay student loans to attract and retain employees in critical positions.
- Exploring legislative proposals to streamline hiring procedures, make noncompetitive conversions of term employees to permanent positions, offer larger recruitment and retention bonuses, expand use of early retirement, and provide authority for permanent and enhanced buyouts.

Knowledge management has an important role to play in NASA's human capital strategy. GAO identified many barriers that hamper knowledge sharing at NASA. Some of the obstacles were (GAO Report 02-195, January 30, 2002):

- Program and project managers believe that senior management support was lacking for sharing lessons learned.
- Significant cultural barriers to knowledge sharing exist beyond the difficulties associated with a stovepiped environment.
- Non-agencywide incentives existed for sharing knowledge.
- Many managers simply lacked time to take part in knowledge sharing activities.
- The sharing of lessons learned was not highly valued across the board.

NASA is addressing these concerns. For NASA to continue its journey in creativity, innovation, and space exploration, knowledge sharing activities within NASA and its partners should be central to NASA's mission and human capital strategy.

Besides NASA, other government agencies are making strategic partnerships integral to their human capital plan. The U.S. Department of Interior (DOI) developed their "Strategic Human Capital Management Plan FY2003–2007" (September 9, 2002, http://www.doi.gov/pfm/human_cap_plan/pdf/entire.pdf), which highlights, in part, the importance for "building partnerships with federal, state, and local governments, citizens, and organizations to address landscape issues that transcend individual agency boundaries." In order for DOI to achieve its vision and performance goals, establishing and outsourcing partnerships is an essential piece of DOI's strategic human capital plan.

The DOI is facing many of the same challenges that other government agencies are experiencing. According to DOI's Human Capital Plan, some of these include an aging workforce; insufficient numbers of people with pivotal business and information technology skills; a need for enhanced law enforcement capability; and a need for negotiating and partnership skills among all employees in the field. The plan indicates that partnerships, science, and effective management are keys to fulfilling DOI's mission and achieving its core mission goals in bureaus and offices throughout the department.

Partnerships with other entities within and outside of the department enhance communication and extend the department's capabilities.

The DOI's five-year human capital plan centers on integrating the department's employment of the "4 Cs" (consultation, communication, cooperation, all in the service of conservation), and managing for excellence. The plan indicates that due to stovepiping there is an inclination towards hoarding knowledge instead of sharing and communicating knowledge. Knowledge management is an important function that needs to be further emphasized throughout the Department.

The Department of Interior indicates the growing need to deploy a sizeable and diverse nonpermanent workforce. For example, in FY2000, the number of volunteer workers was almost three times the number of employees in DOI's paid workforce. Here again, the importance of reaching out to others and partnering is a key part of the human capital strategy and achieving the Department's mission. The plan cites the Golden Gate National Recreation Area as a case study in partnership building. In FY2002, the park brought in $0.83 for every $1 of appropriated funds through its partnership revenue and volunteer programs. In FY2002, 380 Golden Gate employees worked with over 11,000 volunteers in nearly all of its varied programs. The Plan also states that forest health and wildland fire prevention efforts can only be successful through collaboration with states, local governments, tribes, and other partners (http://www.doi.gov/pfm/human_cap_plan/pdf/entire.pdf).

Building strategic partnerships is essential to organizational existence in today and tomorrow's environments. An organization's human capital strategy must encompass the relationships built both internally and externally. In knowledge management lexicon, this is called human capital, structural capital, and social capital. Human capital is the "brainpower" of the employees. Structural capital is the intellectual assets that can't easily be brought home with the employee (e.g., intellectual property rights, patents, certain databases, etc.). Social capital or relationship capital is knowledge from the customers, suppliers, third parties, or outside partners that can then be assimilated into the organization's knowledge base.

In a November 2001 colloquium on "Developing Global Leaders" at the Federal Executive Institute, "global competencies" was cited as a key area for federal leaders to possess. According to the Winter 2002 issue of *The Business of Government* magazine (IBM Business Consulting Services, Arlington, VA), a considerable and growing number of federal agencies are involved in international work. The Social Security Administration has bilateral agreements with eighteen nations. The Environmental Protection Agency, U.S. Department of Agriculture, U.S. Customs Service, the U.S. Geological Survey and many other U.S. federal agencies have relationships and partnerships with foreign counterparts. In a 2001–2002 survey conducted by the Federal Executive Institute, 37 percent of U.S. federal executives reported collaborating with other agencies or organizations on international projects. Dana Brower, Terry Newell, and Peter Ronayne from the U.S. Office of Personnel Management recommend that interagency and public/private partnerships need to be strengthened to provide for global leadership development ("The Imperative of Developing Global Leaders," *The Business of Government* Magazine, Winter 2002).

Developing private-public strategic partnerships has also been acknowledged by the U.S. Army as being important. Major General James Jackson (Commanding General, Military District of Washington, U.S. Army) commented in a radio interview (www.businessofgovernment.org) about the necessity for private sector partnerships: "the Army decided the best way to improve base housing infrastructure is to partner with private firms who build houses." Similarly, he said, "the U.S. Army is good at many things. But some things we're not as good at as the private industry. And so the desire is to get the experts to do the things that they're good at, and let us go back to doing the things we're good at" (www.businessofgovernment.org). In another radio interview, Stephen Perry, the Administrator at General Services Administration (GSA), said that "another part of that reform would be to enable GSA to enter into public-private partnerships" (www.businessofgovernment.org).

University-government partnerships have existed for many years. According to the National Science and Technology Council, "federal support of basic research is focused at universities where the training of young scientists and engineers is advanced synergistically with the creation of new knowledge" (www.ostp.gov/NSTC/html/prd4.html). In President Bill Clinton's Administration, over $12 billion was being invested in universities for research (www.ostp.gov/NSTC/html/prd4.html). Under President George W. Bush, university-government partnerships are also encouraged. For example, President Bush proposed increases in federal investment in assistive technology research and development. According to President Bush's foreword "Fulfilling America's Promise to Americans with Disabilities,"

> *Rehabilitative Engineering Research Centers (RERCs) are recognized as conducting some of the most innovative and high-impact assistive technology research in the Federal Government. The 15 RERCs are housed in universities and other non-profit institutions around the country and focus on a specific area of research—for example, information technology access, prosthetics and orthotics, and technology for children with orthopedic disabilities. To advance research specifically targeted to the disabilities community, the Administration will significantly increase funding for the RERCs. (http://wdsc.doleta.gov/disability/htmldocs/new_freedom.html)*

The National Science Foundation in the United States believes very strongly in partnerships for innovation. According to John Hurt of the National Science Foundation, the U.S. innovation system is evolving due to the increased role of research in innovation, the demise of large corporate basic research laboratories, the increased role of newcomers and small firms, the increased role of academe (research and education), the importance of public funding for research, and the pervasive nature of information technology (http://www.nsf.gov/pubs/2002/nsf02060/nsf02060.htm). According to Hurt, patents granted in the U.S. patent system are increasingly linked to public research, and two-thirds of the cited papers were published by organizations primarily supported by public funding. Various lessons learned have resulted from partnerships between universities, industry, and government (http://www.nsf.gov/pubs/2002/nsf02060/nsf02060.htm):

- Firms that collaborate with universities report that more than 10% of their products resulted from the collaboration.
- Industry wants universities to concentrate on research and education, rather than the development of products.
- Small businesses affiliated with academia are significantly more successful than those that are not.
- The lasting impact of successful state programs has been the development of the intellectual infrastructure for research and education.
- Partnerships between universities and governments and industry and business have been most successful when each partner does what it does best, leaving the remainder of the innovation process to the others.

## USING ONLINE COMMUNITIES TO STRENGTHEN HUMAN CAPITAL

Social networking is a powerful way to bring people closer together. Whether through the informal grapevine or via people of similar interests within and between units, social networks are formed within organizations. One way to capitalize on these networks from a human capital perspective is to establish online communities. Within the knowledge management (KM) field, online communities are probably the most used application of KM for sharing knowledge and building social networks. The World Bank has well over 130 online communities (they call them "thematic groups"). Best Buy, Hallmark, the Federal Aviation Administration, American Management Systems, Computer Sciences Corporation, and many other organizations are actively using online communities.

How do online communities enhance human capital in an organization? First, they help create new relationships and strengthen existing ones by reaching out to others with similar interests for advice, guidance, and support. Second, the online communities should increase employee morale and satisfaction as bonding is strengthened. Last, online communities should allow new insights and increased innovation to be gained through interactions with customers, suppliers, partners, and employees.

Strategically, online communities can greatly enhance partnerships as part of an organization's human capital equation. Hallmark uses them effectively to interact with their customers to gather and share the customers' insights for improved business and customer relationship management processes and ideas for new types of cards. The social capital that is developed through learning from customers enriches the organizational intelligence of the firm.

## Linking with Universities for Stimulating an Organization's Intellectual Capital

One way that organizations can maximize their human capital and intellectual wealth is by partnering with universities. In the 1980s and during the early days of commercialized artificial intelligence, Digital Equipment Corporation (DEC) linked with Carnegie Mellon University for developing expert systems for DEC's applications (such as computer configuration, computer sales assistance, etc.). NASA has actively involved universities throughout the years to contribute to NASA's intellectual capital. For example, the Jet Propulsion Laboratory is really comprised of Cal Tech employees. The Johns Hopkins University Applied Physics Laboratory has been involved as principal investigators on NASA satellite missions. In fact, scientists from universities throughout the world have cooperated with NASA on satellite missions, manned missions, and other NASA projects.

The government should continue to reach out to universities for maximizing the agency's human capital. Through summer faculty fellowship programs, graduate student research programs, co-ops and internships, and other university-government programs, faculty and students can inject some new ideas into the agency and, similarly, professors and students can mutually learn from the government employees.

## What's Ahead?

As outsourcing continues to take a greater role in the federal government, strategic partnerships will become increasingly important as part of the agency's human capital knowledge base. Contractors, other than full-time permanent employees, universities, international partners, and other key groups will contribute significantly to an organization's human capital strategy. It would be very worthwhile to hire recent retirees as part-time retired annuitants or through emeriti programs to play mentoring and knowledge retention roles in the organization. In the years ahead, there certainly will be more nontraditional mechanisms being employed to develop an agency's human capital knowledge base. The future looks bright if organizations maximize, leverage, and synergize all human capital elements comprising an agency's human capital plan.

# TEN

# Strategic Management of Human Capital: The Future

Any chief executive officer will tell you that the competitive edge that his or her organization has over others is its people. People are the key asset that distinguishes one organization from another. The people, and affiliated partnerships, provide the "brainpower" to propel the organization through the waters, either through smooth or choppy tides. As a result of this realization, various communities have been trying to measure the contribution of human capital to an organization. Human resource accounting techniques have been used in the past to measure people's worth. Activity-based costing methods and other financial accounting practices have been applied to measure human capital. The knowledge management community has also been interested in measuring the intellectual capital of an organization. Companies like Skandia publish an annual intellectual capital report to measure their intellectual capital. Researchers like Nick Bontis at McMaster University have even developed models to measure the intellectual capital of a nation.

For organizations to achieve their strategic vision, people will need to be recognized as an asset rather than a cost. Strategic partnerships will continue to be created to maximize the wealth of human capital in an organization. The positions of Chief Human Capital (or People) Officers will most likely be created to spearhead the strategic management of human capital in an agency. Increased emphasis on knowledge management within the government will occur, with many agencies hiring either Chief Knowledge Officers (CKOs) or Knowledge Management Officers. These CKOs will work closely with the Chief Human Capital Officers to help build and nurture a knowledge sharing culture. Increased usage of recent retirees, term appointments, university and corporate relationships, and outsourcing will take place in the government as part of an agency's human capital plan. Improved recruiting and hiring processes will be utilized to attract new employees into public service and retain individuals with critical skills. Legislative reforms will most likely be invoked to help government agencies cope with the ensuing human capital crisis. An emphasis on developing a results-oriented, customer service–centric culture will play a major role in reshaping government agencies.

Government agencies, as well as industry, must be sensitized to the need to include the four pillars of a human capital strategy: competency management, performance management, knowledge management, and change management. Each pillar must be included in an organization's human capital strategic plan. Each pillar has a symbiotic relationship with each other and, when combined, form a powerful structure for building a human capital strategy.

## The Need to Further Leverage Informal Networks in Organizations

Tom Davenport of Accenture and Larry Prusak of IBM believe that 70 to 80 percent of learning is done through informal means. This implies that a personalized approach as opposed to a codified approach to knowledge management and building a learning organization should be a critical part of an organization's human capital strategy. Rob Cross of the University of Virginia and Larry Prusak, in their article "The People Who Make Organizations Go—or Stop" (*Harvard Business Review*, June 2002), present evidence that the real work in organizations is done informally, through personal contacts. Their research indicates that the executives can manage and enhance the effectiveness of these informal networks by focusing their attention on the key role-players in the group. Cross and Prusak feel that there are four common role-players: central connectors, boundary spanners, information brokers, and peripheral specialists. The central connectors link most people in an informal network with one another. Boundary spanners connect an informal network with other parts of the company or with similar networks in other organizations. Information brokers keep the various subgroups in an informal network together. Peripheral specialists are people in an informal network that others can turn to for specialized expertise. Cross and Prusak further believe that it is only after executives openly and systematically start working with informal networks that the groups will become more effective.

## Tapping into the Senior Workforce

According to Alison Wellner's article "Tapping a Silver Mind" (*HR Magazine*, March 2002), 60 percent of older boomers and nearly two-thirds of boomers now 38 to 47 expect to work during retirement. According to this article and data from the U.S. Census Bureau and U.S. Administration on Aging, the projected number of older American workers (age 65 and older) will be 39 million in 2010 and 70 million in 2030. As a result, according to Shari Fryer, the director of research for a strategic HR firm, Drake Beam Morin, HR professionals may need to have new performance incentives tailored to older workers such as opportunities to add vacation time, change work schedules, enhance health benefits, assist in personal development, and others. Organizations, as part of their human capital strategy, should consider the impact of an aging workforce. According to Fryer, MITRE enables older workers to stay in the workforce through "phased retirement, part-time work, sabbaticals, and a 'Reserves at the Ready' program that allows employees with at least of ten years of company service to become part-time on-call employees staffing projects throughout the corporation."

To prepare for the age boom, Wellner and Valerie Pagnelli (of Watson Wyatt Worldwide) discuss some steps that HR should be doing now:

- Analyze your current workforce. Companies should mine employee data to determine turnover patterns and retirement history and create projections five, ten, and twenty years from now.
- Companies should investigate the demographic mix of the community that supplies their workers.
- Conduct qualitative and quantitative research with current older workers to learn how a company could improve its relationship with older workers.
- Provide retirement education workshops to help persuade aging workers to stay on the job.

Certainly, the organization's success is embedded in its people, and organizations and researchers will continue to look at ways to measure human capital. According to Eilene Zimmerman's article "What are Employees Worth?" (*Workforce Magazine,* February 2001), analysts and experts agree that nearly 75 percent of the sources of value in a company are never reported, and we have yet to come up with an accounting system that can record it all. According to Zimmerman, the bottom line is human capital matters when it comes to the bottom line! Saratoga Institute has been measuring the value of human capital for twenty years. They have developed ten measures of human capital management, according to Zimmerman and Jack Fitz-enz (founder of the Institute):

1. *Your most important issues*
2. *Human capital value added:* how do the people in your organization optimize themselves for the good of the company and for themselves?

3. *Human capital return on investment:* ratio of dollars spent on pay and benefits to an adjusted profit figure.
4. *Separation cost (the costs to the organization of people leaving):* the average cost of separation for an employee is at least six months' equivalent of revenue per employee.
5. *Voluntary separation rate*
6. *Total labor cost revenue percent:* total benefit and compensation cost as a percent of organizational revenue.
7. *Total compensation revenue percent:* percent of the organization's revenues that are allocated to the direct costs of the employees.
8. *Training investment factor*
9. *Time to start:* monitoring the time from approval of a requisition until someone is on the job is a strategic indicator of revenue production.
10. *Revenue factor*

Skandia, the Swedish financial services firm, has also been a leader in trying to measure its intellectual capital. It produces the Skandia Navigator report, which looks at the organization from financial, process, human, customer, and renewal and development perspectives. Nuala Beck, a Canadian economist, developed a set of intellectual capital measures:

- *Knowledge ratio:* expresses the number of knowledge workers as a percentage of total employment in an industry, individual company, or organization (measures the "Corporate IQ").
- *Return-on-knowledge assets:* the number of knowledge workers to profit earned.
- *Patent-to-stock price ratio:* the ratio of the number of patents divided by the price of a company's stock.
- *Research-to-development ratio:* the ratio of research dollars spent to the development dollars spent.

- *Research and development (R&D) to patent ratio:* the ratio of R&D investment to number of new patents issued.

Liebowitz has developed a set of factors that affect human capital growth in an organization, as shown in the following list:

**Training and Education (T&E)**
- Formal training of employees
- Formal education of employees
- Mentoring and on-the-job training

**Skills (S)**
- Research skills
- Entre- and intrapreneurship skills
- Retention rates

**Outside Pressures and Environmental Impacts (OP&EI)**
- Industry competition
- Half-life of information in industry
- Demand and supply of those in the field

**Internal and Organizational Culture (I&OC)**
- R&D expenditures of the organization
- Formalized knowledge transfer systems
- Informal knowledge transfer systems
- Interaction with customers and users
- Physical environment and ambiance
- Internal environment within the organization
- Short-term and long-term goals

**Psychological Impacts (PI)**
- Morale
- Creativity and ingenuity
- Stimulation and motivation

Here, human capital growth is a function of T&E + S + OP&EI + I&OC + PI.

In the future, more organizations will continue to develop metrics for measuring their intangible assets.

## Building the "Organizational Intelligence"

Essentially, organizations are striving to build their "organizational intelligence." Organizational intelligence is the collective assemblage of all intelligences that contribute towards building a shared vision, renewal process, and direction for the entity, per Liebowitz's primer, *Building Organizational Intelligence: A Knowledge Management Primer* (CRC Press, 2000). A key part of organizational intelligence is the renewal process in fostering organizational learning within the entity. The ability to transform individual learning into organizational learning is a challenge in the organization. The use of online communities is an important mechanism that organizations are applying to assist in the learning, knowledge preservation, and knowledge sharing and deployment processes. According to Computer Sciences Corporation, there are several good practices for developing communities of practice:

- Focus on a compelling need.
- Give the group visibility (e.g., publicize in newsletters).
- Provide recognition and incentives for participation.
- Tell "real life" stories to highlight the value of sharing.
- Use both face-to-face meetings periodically and online communities to build social capital and trust.
- Get senior management's support and buy-in and have them be advocates to highlight the group to others.
- Provide task assignments for group members.
- Have a facilitator for the CoP (community of practice).
- Make sure group members know their roles.
- Start small and pick the "low hanging fruit" that will likely show success.
- Use Tech Clubs, such as at DaimlerChrysler and Dow Corning Europe.

Organizational learning is an arduous task, especially for large organizations like government agencies. However, to achieve a human capital strategy, organizational learning—especially in the context of knowledge management—must occur. There are several obstacles that make organizational learning difficult, as expressed by the American Productivity and Quality Center's report "If We Only Knew What We Know" (www.apqc.org):

- Organizational structures that promote "silo" thinking, in which locations, divisions, and functions focus on maximizing their own accomplishments and rewards, hoarding information, and thereby suboptimizing the entire organization.
- A culture that values personal technical expertise and knowledge creation over knowledge sharing.
- The lack of contact, relationships, and common perspectives among people who don't work side-by-side.
- An overreliance on transmitting "explicit" rather than "tacit" information.
- Not allowing or rewarding people for taking the time to learn and share and help each other outside of their own small corporate village.

## Knowledge Management Technology

Knowledge management technology is maturing, which will enable an organization to build a knowledge management and human capital infrastructure. According to Ovum in the January 2003 *KMWorld* magazine, the estimated knowledge management and business intelligence software market in 2002 is around $16 billion and is expected to grow to $21 billion in 2006. Ovum indicates that there have been three main phases to knowledge management software thus far. The first phase, during 1998–2000, was the "hype" phase, which could be termed the "Discovery" stage. The second phase, during 2000–2002, was the “accepted” phase, which might be called the “Collaboration” stage. The current phase, from 2003 and beyond, is the “embedded” phase, which is characterized by software “Integration.”

Etienne Wenger produced a report for the Federal CIO Council’s Subcommittee on Knowledge Management in March 2001 on communities of practice and knowledge management software (http://km.gov/documents/Technology_Survey.doc). Some of the popular online community software programs are Intranets.com, Communispace, Groove, and Open Text’s LiveLink. Popular expertise locator software programs include AskMe Enterprise, Tacit Knowledge System’s KnowledgeMail, Sopheon Organik, and Kamoon’s Connect. Often-used taxonomy and high-end knowledge management tools are Autonomy, Semio Stratify (Discovery System), Documentum, Grapevine, Verity, Intraspect, and IBM Lotus’ Knowledge Discovery System. Popular online searchable video software includes Convera, Virage, and Streamsage.

According to the January 2003 *KMWorld* magazine, five key trends in knowledge management to watch are:

- The move toward integrated KM suites (e.g., Documentum/ Plumtree bought e-Room; IBM and Oracle have filled gaps in their KM offerings)
- Collaboration (handle collaboration across the enterprise)
- Expertise location (a high growth area)
- Real-time business information needs: enhance the role of the enterprise portal and integrate the portal with core infrastructure technologies and decision support
- The rise of the semantic enterprise: web services standards will provide the technical basis for integration across the organization

## RECOMMENDATION FOR REFORM

Stephen Barr’s article “Another Volcker Report, Another Shot at Reform” (*The Washington Post*, January 12, 2003), reported on the findings of Paul Volcker, chairman of a private commission on public service:

> *The notion of public service, once a noble calling proudly pursued by the most talented Americans of every generation, draws an indifferent response from today's young people and repels many of the country's leading private citizens . . . Those who enter the civil service often find themselves trapped in a maze of rules and regulations that thwart their personal development and stifle their creativity. The best are underpaid. . . . Too many of the most talented leave the public service too early.*

The Volcker report further states that: "The simple reality is that federal public servants are constrained by their organizational environment. Changes in federal personnel systems will have limited impact if they are not accompanied by significant change in the operating structure of the executive branch." The commission recommends, in part, a reorganization of the U.S. government, higher pay for judges and federal executives, a cut in the number of political appointees, and the elimination of the white collar pay schedule.

As Stephen Barr points out, this second commission report follows a Volcker commission report in 1989 that stated:

> *There is evidence on all sides of an erosion of performance and morale across government in America. Too many of our most talented public servants—those with the skills and dedication that are the hallmarks of an effective career service—are ready to leave. Too few of our brightest young people—these with the imagination and energy that are essential for the future—are willing to join.*

Have we progressed very far since 1989 in addressing this human capital problem? Many believe that we have not! Perhaps the formation of the new Department of Homeland Security will trigger a more detailed look at restructuring the government as a whole. In President Bush's blueprint for government reform (http://www.whitehouse.gov/news/usbudget/blueprint/budix.html), three major themes are highlighted: a citizen-centered government, a results-oriented government, and a market-based government. For making the government more citizen-centered, the reform initiatives cited were:

- Flatten the federal hierarchy
- Use the Internet to create a citizen-centric government
- Create an E-Government fund.

For making the government more results-oriented, President Bush's reform initiatives are (http://www.whitehouse.gov/news/usbudget/blueprint/budix.html):

- Link budget and management decisions to performance
- Ensure financial accountability
- Reduce erroneous payments to beneficiaries and other recipients of government funds
- Use capital planning to improve performance
- Eliminate duplicative and ineffective programs
- Expand the use of performance-based contracts
- Incorporate successful private sector reforms throughout the federal workforce

To make government market-based, the reform initiatives cited by the White House are (http://www.whitehouse.gov/news/usbudget/blueprint/budix.html):

- Make e-procurement the government-wide standard
- Open government activities to competition

## Final Thoughts

We are facing a human capital crisis in the federal government in the United States. The strategic management of human capital is the top government-wide initiative in the President's Management Agenda.

For the health of the government and its workforce, it is critical that agencies use a myriad of approaches to address this human capital dilemma. Certainly, the four key pillars discussed in this book—competency management, performance management, knowledge management, and change management—should form the underlying structure for developing a human capital strategy. Many concepts from the knowledge management field, as expressed throughout this book, can be applied to address the strategic management of human capital in an organization. We must work hard at this issue if we are to produce a citizen-centered, results-oriented, market-based government; develop and nurture its human capital; and create a knowledge sharing culture across the government.

# Case Study: An Operational Study of Knowledge Management Activities at the ABC Foundation

## Introduction

In developing a new strategic plan for looking towards the new century, the ABC Foundation (a pseudonym) stated that its greatest asset is the vast amount of information and knowledge it has to share. As such, knowledge management and knowledge sharing are major commitments for the coming years for the Foundation. One of the reasons for engaging in knowledge management is to increase innovation, thereby contributing towards becoming an innovating, learning organization. Innovative efforts include the search for and the discovery, experimentation, and development of new technologies, new products and/or services, new production processes, and new organizational structures. Organizations that are able to stimulate and improve the knowledge of their human capital are much more prepared to face today's rapid changes and innovate in the domain where they decide to invest and to compete. The success of an innovative product is notoriously connected to research activities and changing orientation. These two elements depend on the development of knowledge levels and the innovative efforts of knowledge workers (Carneiro, 2000).

Innovation processes are becoming more interactive—more dependent on knowledge that is widely distributed—therefore knowledge management is increasingly central. Swan et al. (1999) believe that the community-based model for knowledge management stimulates innovation better than the IT-led model for knowledge management. They believe that the community networking model influences innovation as knowledge for innovation is socially constructed and based on experience. Knowledge management initiatives that encourage active networking are the key to interactive innovation processes.

According to Perez-Bustamante (1999), innovation is a learning process that takes place between scientific research and the market, through which the organization uses scientific and engineering knowledge bases to develop products with the characteristics demanded by the market. Then, the organization has to adapt the new product or process to its internal characteristics and product portfolio. This adaptation requires the development of organizational changes that are fundamentally based on learning processes. These organizational learning processes, which comprise part of the knowledge management life cycle, will affect the agility of an organization in adapting to new techniques and environmental factors and stimulating innovative efforts (Perez-Bustamante, 1999).

Some people, like Debra Amidon with Entovation International (www.entovation.com/innovation/knowinno.htm), have suggested coupling knowledge management with innovation to create "knowledge innovation." Knowledge innovation is the creation, evolution, exchange, and application of new ideas into marketable goods and services for the success of an enterprise, the vitality of a nation's economy, or the advancement of society. Amidon feels that knowledge innovation is one further step on the management performance trajectory than knowledge management—integrating knowledge management with innovation management. Effective knowledge management is a necessary prerequisite, but companies are developing the role of knowledge in their innovation processes (Connor and Gutknecht, 1998). Amidon stresses the need for a community of "knowledge" practice whereby an informal network of people is sharing ideas on the strategic focus of knowledge and developing knowledge in pursuit of common ideas and goals. In looking at R&D generations, we have moved into the fifth generation of "knowledge as the asset," versus the earlier generations of the product as the asset (first), project as the asset (second), enterprise as the asset (third), and customer as the asset (fourth). There are organizations like SCOAP, a not-for-profit organization in Canada, that annually provide awards to organizations for the best knowledge management innovation initiative.

Dougherty (1992) has looked at a practice-centered model of organizational renewal through product innovation. Through her work, she has observed how product innovators gather tacit visceral knowledge and transform it into articulated knowledge. Articulating visceral knowledge relies heavily on the art of direct interpersonal relations with potential users. Glynn (1996) views organizational intelligence as related to innovation. Organizational intelligence is a social outcome and is related to individual intelligence by mechanisms of aggregation. Glynn's work suggests that intrinsic motivation is necessary for creativity and innovation. This type of motivation can be gained by developing communities of practice so that a sharing process is facilitated. This finding is verified by McClure-Wasko and Faraj (2000) as they indicated that intrinsic motivation, versus extrinsic motivation, is why people participate and help others in electronic communities of practice. Kerssens, de Weerd, and Fisscher (1996) also suggest that knowledge management in research and development is essential for stimulating innovation.

Kanter's (1996) extensive fieldwork confirmed that organizations can foster innovation. Key elements to stimulate innovation include close contact with users who are sources of needs, crossfertilization of ideas, high connectivity among workers and functional areas, broadly scoped jobs, coalition building, open communication, crosscutting teams, continuity of personnel, and flexibility to adapt to changing conditions (Agresti, 2000; Alavi and Leidner, 2001). The literature seems to confirm that knowledge management and innovation go hand-in-hand. Being knowledge-based is now one of the most important innovative thrusts for any organization.

This case study will describe the knowledge management activities in ABC Foundation as it strives to become a knowledge leader and an innovating, learning organization. Knowledge management implementation critical success factors will be proposed, and a description of the various knowledge management initiatives at the Foundation will be explained. Afterwards, a discussion on areas that the Foundation needs to strongly consider will be explained in order for the Foundation to reach its strategic knowledge sharing goal.

## Knowledge Management Implementation Critical Success Factors

According to the knowledge management study of thirty-one projects in twenty-four companies conducted by Davenport, De Long, and Beers (1998), the most important factors for successful implementation of knowledge management projects are: having a knowledge-oriented culture; creating an organizational infrastructure that systematically supports knowledge management; finding effective motivational tools; and developing senior management support. These factors contribute towards building a successful knowledge-centric organization.

Building a knowledge-centric organization via a knowledge management framework has several key elements as critical success factors. The basic building blocks are creating an awareness of knowledge management; performing knowledge management benchmarking to see what other similar organizations have done; developing a knowledge taxonomy that serves as a vocabulary and structure in which to construct the knowledge management system; developing a knowledge management strategy; and pinpointing target areas for greatest use of knowledge management activities. Then, the next level involves selecting appropriate knowledge management technologies and tools, developing a knowledge management organizational infrastructure, and building and nurturing online communities of practice (CoP). Afterwards, knowledge management pilots can be conducted and measurements made, along with instituting a change management process within the organization. Finally, full implementation of the knowledge management systems, processes, and practices can be made, while constantly sustaining and extending a knowledge sharing culture.

Agresti (2000) indicates that the knowledge management implementation critical success factors fall into three main areas: leadership, project characteristics, and organizational context. Under *leadership*, top management involvement and commitment are essential and employees must perceive genuine commitment to the goals of the knowledge management initiative through the actions of the organizational leadership. Business users, not the information systems staff, should drive the knowledge management projects. These initiatives should be tied to line-of-business practices (Agresti, 2000).

For *project characteristics*, the knowledge management team needs people with specific skills. The knowledge management team members need to understand the sociological and technological issues associated with knowledge capture, document management, and corporate networked infrastructures (Agresti, 2000). Key success criteria in the *organizational context* are a technological infrastructure and a "knowledge friendly" culture. Knowledge management requires change in behavior and organizational values to allow for a knowledge friendly environment. Also, providing for sustainment is an important success factor for the knowledge management programs to survive (Agresti, 2000).

In order to evaluate how well the knowledge management initiatives are doing, metrics need to be developed. For example, the American Productivity and Quality Center looked at a set of knowledge management indicators that included such measures as:

- *Customer Relationships:* quality customer retention, growth rates.

- *Human Resources:* quality employee retention, rate of investment in intellectual capital (such as training expenditures, employees on sabbatical, employee development plans in progress).
- *Strategic Alliances:* value-added from joint ventures, and associations with learning institutions, customers, suppliers, and competitors.
- *Innovation:* new products/services launched, exited product/service lines, prototypes in test, information value-added to products/services.
- *Process Improvements:* best practices imported from elsewhere, best practices exported to others, cycle time and cost reductions, productivity and quality improvements.

At British Petroleum, they used various knowledge sharing metrics (Lee, 2000):

- Number of links per respondents
- Frequency of advice seeking
- Individuals with highest number of nominations (i.e., identifies the true experts)
- Ratio of internal to external links (how inward-looking or otherwise a business unit is)
- Proportion of total contacts that are inward (how sought after the knowledge of that business unit is)
- Proportion of total contacts that are outward (which business units seek help the most)
- Number of shared documents published
- Number of improvement suggestions made
- Corporate directory coverage
- Number of patents published
- Number of presentations made

For the ABC Foundation, customized measures will need to be developed, such as the improvement in cycle time in getting a grant reviewed, approved, and funded; customer satisfaction in using the e-grants system; increase in colleague and consumer interaction and collaboration via the online communities; development of innovative ideas in the Foundation's core competencies; and others.

## Knowledge Management–Related Initiatives at ABC Foundation

One of the strategic priorities for the Foundation is knowledge access. This knowledge access goal is also highlighted in the Annual Plan for the Foundation. The intended outcomes are to increase accessibility to the Foundation's knowledge about the Foundation's core competencies and to enhance the availability of knowledge in these areas. The strategies used to accomplish these outcomes are: establish the Foundation's knowledge center to serve practitioners and others working in the field; enhance the availability of the Foundation's knowledge on the Internet; and provide leadership to establish a national resource on knowledge, including knowledge-based tools to assist individuals and organizations. The knowledge creation and dissemination strategic thrust will make the Foundation's knowledge more accessible and useful to internal program managers and external practitioners.

The cover of the annual report for ABC Foundation had one phrase listed: "sharing knowledge." As such, a Knowledge Initiative has been created at the Foundation to help in knowledge sharing, creation, and dissemination. According to the CEO of the Foundation, knowledge management will be a part of everyone's job at the Foundation. A major part of this Knowledge Initiative at the Foundation is the development of their knowledge transfer system website. This knowledge transfer system has a number of features including a knowledge library, communities of interest, newsfeeds, e-journals and e-magazines, resource locators, hot topics, links to internal partner pages, best practices, and other features.

According to the Knowledge Initiative Focus Group Report for the Foundation, the following findings and recommendations were made:

- High use of the Internet exists at the Foundation.
- Technology infrastructures vary greatly.
- E-mail and e-mail updates on policy/legislation are useful.
- Just-in-time approaches to learning are used.
- Universities were not identified as sources of information (however, the Foundation's university community partnership initiative allows lessons learned to be shared with industry and universities).
- The knowledge transfer system should be "value-added," provide practical information, and not be used for public relations reasons.
- People rely on established relationships and word of mouth.
- Use mixed media—video, audio, graphics, text, etc.
- Prefer personalized, face-to-face approaches for interaction.
- Need to develop a strategy to foster buy-in and use of the Knowledge Initiative (need to sharply define the customer base).
- Need to better analyze and synthesize information—want summarized information for the users due to time constraints.
- Need to include information about funding sources.

As part of the Knowledge Initiative at the Foundation, there are a number of components that are contributing towards having the Foundation be the knowledge leader in its field. First, the Foundation website contains a wealth of information to help consumers, grant seekers, practitioners, policymakers, researchers, and the media. Search capabilities allow easy access to the Foundation's grants and publications. Online grant submission is also used by first accepting letters of inquiry over the Internet.

Second, the Foundation has been implementing their knowledge transfer system to provide a website to promote innovation, enhance best practices, and build online communities of practice for those interested in the Foundation's core competencies. Through the knowledge transfer system, online communities of interest and practice will be established to have online chats and threaded discussions on key issues.

Third, a Knowledge Initiative Advisory Committee (KIAC) has been established that consists of policymakers, practitioners, academics, and private industry leaders in the Foundation's field. The KIAC meets on a periodic basis to provide guidance towards building the Knowledge Initiative at the Foundation. Focus groups have also been conducted nationwide to gather input from prospective users of the Knowledge Initiative's programs and services. This feedback is instrumental in shaping the knowledge transfer system and the Knowledge Initiative programs.

Fourth, the Foundation has been making active use of its intranet to communicate and share information and knowledge internally. Strategic plans, annual plans, expertise locator (the Foundation's "find anyone"), and a myriad of other materials are available on the intranet. Questions can also be posed over the intranet or bulletin boards in order to exchange and discuss information and knowledge and help build internal communities of practice.

Fifth, the Foundation continues to reach out to its constituencies in developing a collaborative knowledge base in its core competencies. Through its active and well-funded research grants program, the Foundation has developed a vast resource for creating knowledge in its field. Additionally, the Foundation has a number of initiatives, like the University-Community Partnership Initiative, that stimulate ideas and knowledge exchanges between various organizations interested in the housing field. Also, the Foundation publishes journals that serve as important scholarly outlets for generating new knowledge in the Foundation's field.

Sixth, the Foundation is using a myriad of other knowledge sharing techniques to reach out to its constituents. Some of these methods include the Leadership and Knowledge Network, the Knowledge Initiative Speaker Series, online training and education, online consumer outreach network, and an e-grants strategy for online submission, review, and approval of grants electronically. Additionally, the Foundation is providing leadership for creating knowledge links within the Foundation's network of partnerships and structuring research affiliations so as to maximize the Foundation's innovative "virtual think tank" operating style. This is extending the Foundation's knowledge partnerships with universities and think tanks in the field.

Last, the Foundation has been working with knowledge management consultants to help build a conceptual model for knowledge management, develop a knowledge taxonomy for the industry, and assist in the development of the Foundation's knowledge management strategy and online communities.

## Discussion

The ABC Foundation has made impressive steps, as previously highlighted, towards becoming the knowledge leader in its field. In conducting interviews with key individuals in the Foundation, a number of suggestions were made to ensure that the Knowledge Initiative succeeds. These include (Liebowitz, 2001a):

- Ensure that all senior management officials are strongly committed to the Knowledge Initiative and that they will also be actively involved in using the knowledge management systems.
- Develop a knowledge management education program throughout the Foundation so that everyone can better understand the principles of knowledge management and how the knowledge management initiatives will impact their current roles and responsibilities.
- Have an internal knowledge management working or core group consisting of representatives in the Foundation from the

different areas—the representatives will become the "knowledge stewards" in their respective areas in helping to build support and educate their colleagues in knowledge management.

- Use storytelling as a means of sharing tacit knowledge and codify the stories in the knowledge transfer system (storytelling is a popular way of conveying knowledge in the field).
- Develop a standard evaluation process to measure outcomes and effectiveness metrics relating to the knowledge management initiatives.
- Use intelligent agent technology to push relevant lessons learned and material to those within (and perhaps outside) the Foundation and Company.
- Use more crossfunctional teams to cut across functional silos.
- Creating teams could be impeded by the overly formal structure of the organization (even though there are only about 107 Foundation members).
- Need to have a more robust program development function.
- Make sure that these knowledge management initiatives are appropriately resourced.
- Target "breaking/hot" areas of knowledge for online communities and threaded discussions.
- Mine the Foundation's grant database for further creating knowledge and "good-best practices/lessons learned."
- Use intrinsic motivation first for encouraging use of online communities (although, a number of organizations use extrinsic motivation, incorporating learning and knowledge sharing criteria into the individual's annual performance review).
- Develop an ability to have customized portals for employees within the knowledge transfer system.
- Create a comprehensive knowledge taxonomy that would be used for categorizing the content on the knowledge transfer

system as well as for organizing expertise for an expertise locator system.

- Continue to incorporate feedback mechanisms to refine and augment the knowledge transfer system via practitioner, policymaker, media, and academic input.
- Track and share research originating from the grants and link with the Foundation's strategic planning process.
- Continue to nurture a knowledge sharing environment (e.g., continuing to share weekly reports across the Foundation).
- Look for better ways of mining the institutional knowledge of those in the Foundation (i.e., the tacit knowledge) to get it into the knowledge transfer system (e.g., may want to use knowledge discovery techniques, web-based expert systems, or online searchable video technologies).

Besides the interviews, a review was made of the internal documents relating to the knowledge management efforts underway and proposed at the Foundation. A number of key areas were only briefly mentioned but in the end will determine the success of the knowledge management initiatives at the Foundation. First, knowledge management is 80 to 90 percent people and culture, and 10 to 20 percent technology. Some minor reference to the need for organizational change management was mentioned in the internal documents, but this should be a well-conceived major component of the knowledge management efforts. Developing a strategy for encouraging and building a knowledge sharing culture, including knowledge sharing proficiencies, techniques, and processes, is a critical component that is being overlooked in the current documents. Second, a guiding principle mentioned in the New Century Initiative was to have measurable results. This is a key area, and metrics for knowledge sharing and demonstrating the success of the knowledge management efforts need to be formalized. Third, mention was made of the need for developing knowledge-based tools for practitioners. This will also provide a value-added benefit in the form of web-based expert systems, decision support systems, and other decision analysis tools.

## Knowledge Sharing and Metrics

The mantra among the knowledge management community is that 80 percent of knowledge management is people and culture and 20 percent is technology. A key component of the people and culture factors deals with encouraging a knowledge sharing environment within the organization (Liebowitz, 1999). Kochikar (2000) has developed a knowledge management maturity model whereby the highest level is "Sharing." This level involves reaching the institutionalization of a culture of sharing whereby sharing becomes second nature to all. Organizational boundaries are rendered irrelevant and knowledge flows frictionlessly (Kochikar, 2000).

Xerox's reputation has been built on a strong knowledge sharing culture. Xerox's Eureka system contains many thousands of tips to help repair technicians worldwide who repair copiers at client sites. At Xerox, knowledge sharing has become part of a fabric inside the company for all employees (Hickins, 1999). Dow Corning has created clubs to promote research and development interaction for knowledge sharing purposes (Easton and Parbhoo, 1998). Many organizations like American Management Systems have created Corporate Knowledge Centers in core competency areas to encourage online communities of practice for increased knowledge sharing (Preece, 2000). Lockheed-Martin applies knowledge sharing by matching the type of knowledge with the right transfer method (Dixon, 2000).

According to The Delphi Group (Hickins, 1999), a study of more than 700 U.S. companies showed that the majority of corporate knowledge is in employees' brains, which presents a challenge in trying to encourage the sharing of this knowledge. About 12 percent of the corporate knowledge was in electronic knowledge bases, 42 percent in employees' brains, 26 percent in paper documents, and 20 percent in electronic documents. In order to elicit and represent the knowledge in people's heads in a formal way, the knowledge acquisition bottleneck (from the days of knowledge engineering) plays a critical role (Liebowitz, 2001b and 2001c; Schreiber et al., 2000). The knowledge engineering paradox states that the more expert an individual, the more compiled is his or her knowledge, and the harder it is to extract this knowledge. This makes knowledge sharing a challenging task, but an organization can promote and nurture its knowledge sharing culture by installing knowledge sharing measures within a motivate-and-reward structure within an organization.

Several organizations already have developed knowledge sharing proficiencies in order to further encourage the use of knowledge sharing within the organization and externally to the organization's customers (Liebowitz and Chen, 2001). The World Bank has learning and knowledge sharing criteria as part of its employees' annual job performance review. American Management Systems evaluates employees partly on how well they contribute to the organization's knowledge repositories and what is the value-added benefit derived from applying the knowledge from these repositories (Andriessen and Tissen, 2000). Gemini Consulting has similar measures for knowledge sharing as part of its employees' performance review.

In order to leverage employee know-how, organizations have found that developing knowledge sharing proficiencies for the organization and incorporating these proficiencies as part of the employee's annual appraisal seems to be a necessary step in helping to build and jump-start a knowledge sharing culture. As the knowledge sharing process becomes institutionalized over time, the culture for knowledge sharing will become a natural occurrence in the organization.

## Knowledge Sharing Proficiencies

Before creating knowledge sharing proficiencies, we must first provide a definition for a "knowledge sharing proficiency." A knowledge sharing proficiency is an attribute that allows the creation of knowledge to take place through an exchange of ideas, expressed either verbally or in some codified way. Some organizations like Johnson & Johnson and the World Bank have knowledge fairs geared to promoting an increase in knowledge sharing and generating new colleague-to-colleague relationships for better transfer of tacit knowledge. A number of organizations have already created knowledge sharing as a guiding principle for the organization. For example, the Public Service Commission in Canada has "Knowledge, Information, and Data Should Be Shared" as one of their four guiding principles.

The World Bank, which wants to be known as the Knowledge Bank, includes learning and knowledge sharing factors as part of its annual performance evaluation. These factors include: open to new ideas and continuous learning; shares own knowledge, learns from others, and applies knowledge in daily work; builds partnerships for learning and knowledge sharing. In a university setting, Liebowitz and Chen (2001) developed knowledge sharing proficiencies within the Information Systems Department to consist of the following:

**Collaboration, in the Form Of**

- Joint proposals/papers one has written with colleagues within and outside the department
- Co-Principal Investigators on funded research efforts
- Participation in research teams with team members from faculty/students in the Department
- Consulting engagements with faculty/students in the Department
- Joint teaching in or giving guest lectures to colleagues' courses (e.g., Honors courses, filling in for others if colleague is out of town, etc.)
- Mentoring colleagues in the Department and providing lessons learned to colleagues
- Letting your colleagues teach courses that you normally teach, especially if it can advance their area of research (i.e., eliminating the philosophy that an individual faculty member "owns" a course)

**Thinking of We, Not Me**

- Circulating articles and special issue announcements that may interest other colleagues in the Department

- Circulating announcements for conferences and RFPs (request for proposals) to colleagues, and putting together joint sessions at conferences
- Engaging in activities to help strengthen the Department versus ones that enhance individual achievement
- Offering appropriate colleagues in the Department to write invited papers if one is unable to do so
- Offering to others a chance to review papers for journals if in the colleague's area of specialization
- Being proactive in Department and University Activities (e.g., attending IT company briefings, meeting IT-related company CEOs, attending IT-related seminars, etc.)
- Letting department faculty and students use one's lab for research appropriate to that lab's focus (versus the attitude that this is "my" lab)
- Providing leads to colleagues for possible research or consulting
- Providing leads to students for jobs and calling personal contacts to allow students to get their foot in the door

Other possible knowledge sharing proficiencies could include: the number of new colleague-to-colleague relationships spawned; the reuse rate of "frequently accessed/reused" knowledge; the number of key concepts that are converted from tacit to explicit knowledge in the knowledge repositories and used by members of the organization; the dissemination of knowledge sharing (i.e., distribution of knowledge) to appropriate individuals; the number of new ideas generating innovative products or services; the number of lessons learned and best practices applied to create value-added; the number of "apprentices" that one mentors, and the success of these apprentices as they mature in the organization (Liebowitz and Suen, 2000; Housel and Bell, 2001).

The U.S. Department of Navy is embracing knowledge management and knowledge sharing principles to transform itself into a knowledge-centric organization. As the sharing of information and knowledge becomes embedded in day-to-day activities, the flow and change of best practices should increase, providing the fluid for true process improvement. In addition, the high visibility of content areas across the organization facilitates the exchange of new ideas regarding process change.

## A Knowledge Sharing Effectiveness Inventory

Over the years, there have been a series of various instruments to assess knowledge management and organizational effectiveness. Some of these instruments include the KMAT (Knowledge Management Assessment Tool) by the American Productivity & Quality Center, Expedient Knowledge Inventory by Strategy 1st, the Organizational Effectiveness Inventory by Human Synergistics, Inc., and the Learning Effectiveness Index by CapitalWorks. These instruments broadly cover elements of how well an organization is learning and applying its knowledge, but they do not specifically look at the issues of knowledge sharing effectiveness for potentially building knowledge sharing proficiencies for an organization.

In order to fill this vacuum, Liebowitz and Chen (2001) developed a knowledge sharing effectiveness inventory that consists of twenty-five questions that are divided into four parts. The first part deals with "Communications Flow," which tries to assess how knowledge and communication exchanges are captured and disseminated throughout the organization. The second part examines the "Knowledge Management Environment," which looks at internal cultural factors related to knowledge management within the organization. The third part deals with "Organizational Facilitation" which assesses the sophistication of the knowledge management infrastructure and knowledge sharing capability within the organization. The last part deals with "Measurement," which assesses the likelihood of knowledge sharing and knowledge management being successful within the organization. The Knowledge Sharing Effectiveness Inventory is shown in the following table.

*Knowledge Sharing Effectiveness Inventory*

This questionnaire has been developed by Dr. Jay Liebowitz and Yan Chen in the Laboratory for Knowledge Management at the University of Maryland–Baltimore County. Kindly mark a response for each statement. The results will be used to determine knowledge sharing proficiencies and effectiveness at the ABC Foundation. Thank you for your help.

| | *Strongly Agree* | *Agree* | *Neutral* | *Disagree* | *Strongly Disagree* |
|---|---|---|---|---|---|
| ABOUT COMMUNICATION | | | | | |
| 1. Key expertise is often captured in an online way in my organization. | | | | | |
| 2. I get appropriate lessons learned sent to me in areas where I can benefit. | | | | | |
| 3. I usually have time to chat informally with my colleagues. | | | | | |
| 4. Individualized learning is usually transformed into organizational learning through documenting this knowledge into our organization's knowledge repository. | | | | | |
| ABOUT KM ENVIRONMENT | | | | | |
| 5. There are many knowledge fairs/exchanges within my organization to spawn new colleague-to-colleague relationships. | | | | | |
| 6. There are lessons learned and best practices repositories within my organization. | | | | | |
| 7. We have a mentoring program within my organization. | | | | | |

*Knowledge Sharing Effectiveness Inventory* (continued)

| | *Strongly Agree* | *Agree* | *Neutral* | *Disagree* | *Strongly Disagree* |
|---|---|---|---|---|---|
| 8. We have Centers of Excellence in our organization whereby you can qualify to become a member/affiliate of the Center. | | | | | |
| 9. We typically work in teams or groups. | | | | | |
| 10. Our main product is our knowledge. | | | | | |
| 11. I feel that we have a knowledge sharing culture within our organization versus a knowledge hoarding one. | | | | | |
| 12. We have a high percentage of teams with shared incentives whereby the team members share common objectives and goals. | | | | | |
| 13. There are online communities of practice in my organization where we can exchange views and ideas. | | | | | |
| ABOUT ORGANIZATIONAL FACILITATION | | | | | |
| 14. I am promoted and rewarded based upon my ability to share my knowledge with others. | | | | | |
| 15. There is an adequate budget for professional development and training in my organization. | | | | | |
| 16. Success, failure, or war stories are systematically collected and used in my organization. | | | | | |

*Knowledge Sharing Effectiveness Inventory* (continued)

| | *Strongly Agree* | *Agree* | *Neutral* | *Disagree* | *Strongly Disagree* |
|---|---|---|---|---|---|
| 17. The measurement system in my organization incorporates intellectual and customer capital, as well as the knowledge capital of our products or services. | | | | | |
| 18. We have the technological infrastructure to promote a knowledge sharing environment within our organization. | | | | | |
| 19. We typically have integrated assignments where the number of projects in which more than one department participates occurs. | | | | | |
| 20. We have internal surveys on teaming, which surveys employees to see if the departments are supporting and creating opportunities for one another. | | | | | |
| 21. We track the degree to which the organization is entering team-based relationships with other business units, organizations, or customers. | | | | | |
| 22. The organization's office layout is conducive to speaking with my colleagues and meeting people. | | | | | |
| ABOUT MEASUREMENT | | | | | |
| 23. The reuse rate of "frequently accessed/reused" knowledge in my organization is high. | | | | | |

*Knowledge Sharing Effectiveness Inventory* (continued)

| | *Strongly Agree* | *Agree* | *Neutral* | *Disagree* | *Strongly Disagree* |
|---|---|---|---|---|---|
| 24. The distribution of knowledge to appropriate individuals in my organization is done actively on a daily basis. | | | | | |
| 25. New ideas generating innovative products or services are a frequent occurrence in my organization. | | | | | |

## Analysis of the Knowledge Sharing Effectiveness Inventory as Applied to the ABC Foundation

The Knowledge Sharing Effectiveness Inventory was distributed both in hard copy at an ABC Foundation all-hands staff meeting, as well as sent electronically to all employees in the Foundation. We received 58 completed surveys out of 107 Foundation members, giving a response rate of 54 percent. The following table shows the percentage results from the completed surveys.

| | *Strongly Agree* | *Agree* | *Neutral* | *Disagree* | *Strongly Disagree* |
|---|---|---|---|---|---|
| ABOUT COMMUNICATION | | | | | |
| 1. Key expertise is often captured in an online way in my organization. | 2% | 17% | 32% | 37% | 12% |
| 2. I get appropriate lessons learned sent to me in areas where I can benefit. | 2% | 19% | 20% | 47% | 12% |
| 3. I usually have time to chat informally with my colleagues. | 14% | 38% | 21% | 21% | 7% |

| | *Strongly Agree* | *Agree* | *Neutral* | *Disagree* | *Strongly Disagree* |
|---|---|---|---|---|---|
| 4. Individualized learning is usually transformed into organizational learning through documenting this knowledge into our organization's knowledge repository. | 2% | 12% | 24% | 45% | 17% |
| ABOUT KM ENVIRONMENT | | | | | |
| 5. There are many knowledge fairs/exchanges within my organization to spawn new colleague-to-colleague relationships. | 4% | 36% | 10% | 38% | 12% |
| 6. There are lessons learned and best practices repositories within my organization. | 7% | 34% | 19% | 33% | 7% |
| 7. We have a mentoring program within my organization. | 4% | 4% | 17% | 48% | 27% |
| 8. We have Centers of Excellence in our organization whereby you can qualify to become a member/affiliate of the Center. | 0% | 7% | 13% | 40% | 40% |
| 9. We typically work in teams or groups. | 7% | 50% | 23% | 18% | 2% |
| 10. Our main product is our knowledge. | 12% | 27% | 26% | 26% | 9% |
| 11. I feel that we have a knowledge sharing culture within our organization versus a knowledge hoarding one. | 2% | 26% | 26% | 41% | 5% |

| | *Strongly Agree* | *Agree* | *Neutral* | *Disagree* | *Strongly Disagree* |
|---|---|---|---|---|---|
| 12. We have a high percentage of teams with shared incentives whereby the team members share common objectives and goals. | 0% | 29% | 31% | 36% | 4% |
| 13. There are online communities of practice in my organization where we can exchange views and ideas. | 2% | 29% | 26% | 31% | 12% |
| ABOUT ORGANIZATIONAL FACILITATION | | | | | |
| 14. I am promoted and rewarded based upon my ability to share my knowledge with others. | 2% | 13% | 24% | 41% | 20% |
| 15. There is an adequate budget for professional development and training in my organization. | 21% | 55% | 9% | 13% | 2% |
| 16. Success, failure, or war stories are systematically collected and used in my organization. | 0% | 12% | 23% | 46% | 19% |
| 17. The measurement system in my organization incorporates intellectual and customer capital, as well as the knowledge capital of our products or services. | 5% | 14% | 27% | 40% | 14% |
| 18. We have the technological infrastructure to promote a knowledge sharing environment within our organization. | 12% | 50% | 12% | 19% | 7% |

| | *Strongly Agree* | *Agree* | *Neutral* | *Disagree* | *Strongly Disagree* |
|---|---|---|---|---|---|
| 19. We typically have integrated assignments where the number of projects in which more than one department participates occurs. | 5% | 36% | 30% | 24% | 5% |
| 20. We have internal surveys on teaming, which surveys employees to see if the departments are supporting and creating opportunities for one another. | 0% | 10% | 10% | 54% | 26% |
| 21. We track the degree to which the organization is entering team-based relationships with other business units, organizations, or customers. | 0% | 8% | 22% | 44% | 26% |
| 22. The organization's office layout is conducive to speaking with my colleagues and meeting people. | 5% | 31% | 28% | 22% | 14% |
| ABOUT MEASUREMENT | | | | | |
| 23. The reuse rate of "frequently accessed/reused" knowledge in my organization is high. | 2% | 13% | 51% | 31% | 3% |
| 24. The distribution of knowledge to appropriate individuals in my organization is done actively on a daily basis. | 2% | 17% | 33% | 41% | 7% |
| 25. New ideas generating innovative products or services are a frequent occurrence in my organization. | 7% | 38% | 33% | 14% | 8% |

In terms of communication, 52 percent of those surveyed felt that they usually have time to chat informally with colleagues. This is an important attribute for building a knowledge sharing culture. This personalized approach can help the exchange of tacit knowledge between individuals, and informal learning through these exchanges can account for 70 to 80 percent of learning, according to Larry Prusak with the IBM Institute of Knowledge Management. The Foundation, however, needs to enhance its codification strategy in terms of capturing key expertise in an online way. Only 19 percent felt that this was being done effectively. The knowledge transfer system initiative should greatly facilitate codifying key expertise via its best practices, lessons learned, and online community components. The Foundation might also consider using intelligent agent technology within their knowledge transfer system to push lessons learned to appropriate individuals who could benefit from these lessons in the organization (only 21 percent said this was currently being done). Transforming individualized learning into organizational learning will be enhanced by the knowledge transfer system, as only 14 percent said that this was being done well currently.

In terms of the knowledge management environment, the Foundation respondents generally acknowledge that the Foundation's main product is knowledge (39 percent agreed, 26 percent neutral). A team-based approach is well-recognized and applied in the Foundation, and there appear to be opportunities to share and exchange knowledge in various informal settings (e.g., company picnic, etc.). Even though the opportunities for knowledge sharing exist, only 28 percent felt that a knowledge sharing culture is present at the Foundation. Prior to the knowledge transfer system, the Knowledge Exchange is on the Foundation's intranet to allow online threaded discussions. Unfortunately, very few people have contributed and used this capability to date. Additionally, only 7 percent agreed that a mentoring program exists within the Foundation. The Foundation may want to consider a formal mentoring program to improve the sharing and exchange of tacit knowledge and encouraging a knowledge sharing culture. Systematic job rotations might also be used to encourage a better understanding of the Foundation's core activities and promote interdisciplinary dialogue. Forty-one percent felt that best practices and lessons learned repositories exist in the Foundation, which is a positive sign towards building a knowledge sharing environment.

In terms of organizational facilitation for developing a knowledge management capability, there are a number of positive signs: 76 percent felt an adequate budget exists for training and development (this is excellent, indicating the further recognition for and development of intellectual capital); 62 percent felt the technological infrastructure to promote knowledge sharing is in place; 41 percent felt that there are crossfunctional, integrated teams being used; and 36 percent felt that the office layout is conducive to speaking with colleagues and meeting people. The Foundation may want to consider revising its motivation and reward system to include learning and knowledge sharing criteria. Only 15 percent felt they were rewarded and promoted based upon their ability to share their knowledge with others. In order to nurture a knowledge sharing culture, the Foundation should consider systematically collecting success, failure, and war stories in the knowledge transfer system, and using "storytelling" as a means for knowledge sharing.

In terms of measurement, 15 percent felt that they typically reused knowledge from others in the Foundation. A low 19 percent felt that knowledge was actively distributed to individuals in the Foundation. On a positive note, 45 percent felt that new ideas generating innovative products or services are a frequent occurrence in the Foundation.

In assessing the four areas of the knowledge sharing effectiveness inventory, the following ratings are deduced based upon the survey results:

- Communication: C–/D+
- Knowledge Management Environment: C
- Organizational Facilitation: C
- Measurement: C

Overall, the Foundation is currently performing at a "C" knowledge sharing level, on a scale of A to F. Even though this may indicate an "average" knowledge sharing performance level, the Foundation will quickly be improving its knowledge sharing effectiveness through its Knowledge Initiative. Additionally, in the author's experience, ABC Foundation scored better than others in this knowledge sharing survey, and is on the right path towards meeting its strategic theme of "sharing knowledge." As a word of caution, however, the Foundation should concentrate on the people, process, and cultural issues relating to knowledge management versus simply the technology issues.

## Summary

"Knowledge sharing" is the key theme for the Foundation. The Knowledge Initiative that is underway at the Foundation is one of the highest priorities (if not the highest) at ABC Foundation, as expressed by the CEO of the Foundation. As evidenced by the surveys and as expressed in the interviews, building and nurturing a knowledge sharing culture at the Foundation is a critical success factor for achieving the strategic goals of the Foundation. This case study tried to assess the level of knowledge sharing in the Foundation to be used as a baseline, and to present some key ideas in developing knowledge sharing proficiencies and linking knowledge management to innovation. Also, critical success factors were proposed for the Foundation and other organizations to follow. It is hoped that this paper will help the Foundation towards reaching its strategic goals in the knowledge management area.

## References

Agresti, W. (2000). "Knowledge management." *Advances in Computers* (vol. 53, annual).

Alavi, M., and D. Leidner (2001). "Knowledge Management and Knowledge Management Systems: Conceptual Foundations and Research Issues." *MIS Quarterly* (vol. 25, no. 1).

Andriessen, D., and R. Tissen (2000). *Weightless Wealth.* London: Prentice Hall Financial Times.

Carneiro, A. (2000). "How Does Knowledge Management Influence Innovation and Competitiveness?" *Journal of Knowledge Management* (vol. 4, no. 2).

Connor, D., and M. Gutknecht (1998). "Helping Clients Harness Knowledge to Drive Innovation." Proceedings of the 2nd International Conference on Practical Aspects of Knowledge Management, ed. U. Reimer. Basel, Switzerland.

Davenport, T., D. De Long, and M. Beers (1998). "Successful Knowledge Management Projects." *Sloan Management Review* (vol. 39, no. 2, Winter).

Davenport, T., and L. Prusak (1998). *Working Knowledge.* Cambridge, MA: Harvard Business School Press.

Dixon, N. (2000). "The Insight Track." *People Management* (vol. 6, no. 4, February 17).

Dougherty, D. (1992). "A Practice-Centered Model of Organizational Renewal through Product Innovation." *Strategic Management Journal* (vol. 13).

Easton, T., and B. Parbhoo (1998). "Clubs Promote R&D Interaction at Dow Corning." *Research Technology Management* (vol. 41, no. 1, January/February).

Glynn, M. (1996). "Innovative Genius: A Framework for Relating Individual and Organizational Intelligences to Innovation." *Academy of Management Review* (vol. 21, no. 4).

Hawryszkiewycz, I. (1999). "Knowledge Sharing through Workspace Networks." 1999 Proceedings of the SIGCPR Conference, Association for Computing Machinery Press, NY.

Hickins, M. (1999). "Xerox Shares Its Knowledge." *Management Review* (vol. 88, no. 8, September).

Housel, T., and A. Bell (2001). Measuring and Managing Knowledge, McGraw Hill, NY.

Kanter, R. M. (1996). "When a Thousand Flowers Bloom: Structural, Collective, and Social Conditions for Innovation in Organizations." Knowledge Management and Organizational Design, ed. P. Myers, Boston: Butterworth-Heinemann.

Kerssens, I., P. de Weerd, and O. Fisscher (1996). "Describing the Issues of Knowledge Management in R&D: Towards a Communication and Analysis Tool." *R&D Management Journal* (vol. 26, no. 3).

Kochikar, V. (2000). "The Knowledge Management Maturity Model—A Staged Framework for Leveraging Knowledge." Proceedings of the KMWorld 2000 Conference, Information Today, Inc., New Jersey, September.

Lee, L. L. (2000). "Knowledge Sharing Metrics for Large Organizations." *Knowledge Management: Classic and Contemporary Works*, D. Morey, M. Maybury, and B. Thuraisingham, eds., Cambridge, MA: MIT Press.

Liebowitz, J., ed. (1999). *The Knowledge Management Handbook*. Boca Raton, FL: CRC Press.

Liebowitz, J. (2001a). Interviews with key individuals in the ABC Foundation.

Liebowitz, J. (2001b). *Knowledge Management: Learning from Knowledge Engineering*. Boca Raton, FL: CRC Press.

Liebowitz, J. (2001). "Lessons Learned in Developing Knowledge Management Strategies for the Government." KM World, Information Today, Inc., January.

Liebowitz, J., and Y. Chen (2001c). "Developing Knowledge Sharing Proficiencies." *Knowledge Management* Review (vol. 3, no. 6, January/February).

Liebowitz, J., and I. Megbolugbe (2003). "A Set of Frameworks to Aid the Project Manager in Conceptualizing and Implementing Knowledge Management Initiatives," International Journal of Project Management (vol. 21, no. 3, April).

Liebowitz, J., and C. Suen (2000). "Developing Knowledge Management Metrics for Measuring Intellectual Capital." *Journal of Intellectual Capital* (vol. 1, no. 1).

McLure-Wasko, M., and S. Faraj (2000). "It Is What One Does: Why People Participate and Help Others in Electronic Communities of Practice." *Strategic Information Systems Journal* (vol. 9, no. 2 and 3).

Perez-Bustamante, G. (1999). "Knowledge Management In Agile Innovative Organizations." *Journal of Knowledge Management* (vol. 3, no. 1).

Preece, J. (2000). *Online Communities: Designing for Sociability and Usability*. London, UK: John Wiley.

Schreiber, G., H. Akkermans, A. Anjewierden, R. de Hoog, N. Shadbolt, W. van de Velde, and B. Wielinga (2000). *Knowledge Engineering and Management: The CommonKADS Approach*. Cambridge, MA: MIT Press.

Swan, J., S. Newell, H. Scarbrough, and D. Hislop (1999). "Knowledge Management and Innovation: Networks and Networking." *Journal of Knowledge Management* (vol. 3, no. 4).

United States General Accounting Office

# GAO

Ranking Member, Subcommittee on Oversight of Government Management, Restructuring, and the District of Columbia, Committee on Governmental Affairs, U.S. Senate

**September 2001**

# HUMAN CAPITAL

## Practices That Empowered and Involved Employees

# Contents


Letter 173

Results In Brief 174
Background 177
Scope And Methodology 181
Six Key Practices Helped Empower And Involve Employees 183
Agencies Addressed Barriers To Efforts That Empowered And Involved Employees 200
Agencies Cited Examples Of Performance Improvements 204
Conclusions 207
Agency Comments 209

Related GAO Products 211

**United States General Accounting Office**
**Washington, D.C. 20548**

September 14, 2001

The Honorable George V. Voinovich
Ranking Member
Subcommittee on Oversight of Government
Management, Restructuring, and the District of Columbia
Committee on Governmental Affairs
United States Senate

Dear Senator Voinovich:

People are the federal government's most valuable asset in managing for results, and you have emphasized the importance of empowering and involving employees to help agencies achieve their goals and improve government operations. As our studies of private and public sector organizations have shown, high-performing organizations focus on valuing and investing in their employees–human capital–and on aligning their "people policies" to support organizational performance goals. However, strategic human capital management is a pervasive challenge in the federal government, and is one of the governmentwide areas that we have identified as high risk.[1]

In addition, the Administration's emphasis on workforce planning and restructuring will require federal agencies to examine how they can flatten their organizational hierarchy and improve their work processes. The Office of Management and Budget's May 8, 2001, bulletin called for agencies to use workforce planning to redistribute higher-level positions to front-line, service delivery positions that interact with citizens.[2] Effective workforce planning and restructuring efforts will build upon implementation of the Government Performance and Results Act of 1993 (GPRA) to address results-oriented goals, improve performance, and assure accountability. To optimize the provision of services to citizens, it is crucial that employees understand the connection between their daily work activities and the results their organizations seek to achieve.

---

[1] *High-Risk Series: An Update* (GAO-01-263, Jan. 2001).

[2] *Office of Management and Budget, Bulletin No. 01–07, Workforce Planning and Restructuring, May 8, 2001.*

At your request, this report examines selected experiences five agencies have had in implementing practices that helped empower or involve front-line employees. Our objectives were to (1) identify and provide examples of the key practices agencies used to empower and involve employees, (2) identify some of the barriers that these agencies experienced and strategies they used to address them, and (3) provide examples of reported performance improvements from empowering and involving employees. As agreed, we have examined selected employee empowerment and involvement practices at specific components within the Federal Aviation Administration (FAA), the Federal Emergency Management Agency (FEMA), the Internal Revenue Service (IRS), the Office of Personnel Management (OPM), and the Veteran's Benefits Administration (VBA). The practices we examined at specific agency components were selected from those initiatives agency officials identified that had, in their view, successfully empowered and involved employees.

## Results In Brief

The organizations we reviewed used six key practices in the initiatives that we reviewed to empower and involve employees. Figure 1 identifies the practices and provides some examples of how the organizations used them.

Figure 1: Six Practices Used to Help Empower and Involve Employees

- **Demonstrating top leadership commitment.** Top leadership commitment is crucial in instilling a common vision across the organization and creating an environment that is receptive to innovation. Leaders of the agency organizations we reviewed envisioned needed changes, communicated openly with employees, and instituted organizational changes. For example, the Director of the FAA Logistics Center decided that the Center needed to operate more like a private sector business. He met in open forums with employees to discuss his vision and, with the help of employees and union representatives, reorganized the Center.

- **Engaging employee unions.** Effective labor-management relations help to achieve consensus and solve problems expeditiously. In some cases the unions participated in pre-decisional discussions with agency management before changes were implemented. For example, IRS involved its employees' union in pre-decisional discussions a bout proposed new policies.

- **Training employees to enhance their knowledge, skills, and abilities.** All five agencies provided formal or on-the-job training to employees to support the changes that were being made. For example, OPM provided on-the-job cross training to a retirement processing team so that the team could adjudicate retirement claims under both the Civil Service Retirement System (CSRS) and the Federal Employees' Retirement System (FERS).

- **Using employee teams to help accomplish agency missions.** All five agencies used teams to help accomplish agency missions. Teams helped flatten organizations by merging divisions and enhanced flexibility in meeting job demands. For example, VBA regional offices created self-directed employee teams and merged divisions to process veterans' benefits claims from beginning to end. Team members learned new skills and had more flexibility to help each other accomplish tasks.

- **Involving employees in planning and sharing performance information.** The agencies involved employees to varying degrees in planning and shared performance information with them. For example, one IRS division used an employee team to help develop its strategic plan and shared performance information. One way that FAA's Logistics center shared performance information was by posting performance data in charts, graphs, and tables throughout the building so employees could see the Center's progress toward achieving organizational goals.

- **Delegating authorities to front-line employees.** Employees at each of the agencies had been delegated authorities. In some instances employees were formally authorized to approve specified dollar levels of program assistance or procurements. For example, FEMA's public assistance coordinators were authorized to approve up to $100,000 in financial assistance to citizens adversely affected by natural disasters or other emergencies. In other instances, teams of employees were provided new authorities to make decisions related to their work processes, workloads, training needs, and work schedules.

For the initiatives we reviewed, the agencies undertook changes that represented a significant shift from their traditional operations and, as such, encountered organizational and cultural barriers that needed to be overcome as they sought to empower and involve employees. These barriers included a lack of trust, resistance to change and lack of buy-in from front-line employees and managers, and a variety of implementation issues, such as workload demands. The agencies developed strategies to address these barriers, such as maintaining open communication and reassigning and hiring personnel. Managers and employees adapted to the changes at their agencies over time, particularly once they perceived benefits, such as improved communication, from the new practices.

In implementing the practices to empower and involve employees, agencies identified a range of examples to demonstrate the performance improvements these efforts have accomplished. Performance improvements cited included increased efficiency and improved customer satisfaction. For example, operating as a team has allowed FAA's Logistics Center to substantially reduce the time needed to make emergency radar repairs.

FAA, IRS, OPM, and VBA generally agreed with the contents of this report. FEMA did not comment on the report.

## Background

No management issue facing federal agencies could be more critical to their ability to serve the American people than their approach to strategic human capital management, including attracting, retaining, and motivating their employees. High-performing organizations in the private and public sectors have long understood the relationship between effective "people management" and organizational success. However, the federal government, which has often acted as if federal employees were costs to be cut rather than assets to be valued, has only recently received its wake-up call. As our January 2001 Performance and Accountability Series reports made clear, serious federal human capital shortfalls are now eroding the ability of many federal agencies—and threatening the ability of others—to economically, efficiently, and effectively perform their missions.[3] The problem lies not with federal employees themselves, but with the lack of effective leadership and management, along with the lack of a strategic approach to marshaling, managing, and maintaining the human capital needed for government to discharge its responsibilities and deliver on its promises.[4]

All five of the agencies we reviewed have experienced challenges in managing their human capital. Each has implemented management changes in response to the challenges they face, including implementing strategies to empower and involve employees.

---

[3] *Performance and Accountability Series—Major Management Challenges and Program Risks: A Governmentwide Perspective* (GAO-01-241, Jan. 2001). In addition, see the accompanying 21 reports, numbered GAO-01-242 through GAO-01-262 on specific agencies.

[4] *Human Capital: Meeting the Governmentwide High-Risk Challenge* (GAO-01-357T, Feb. 1, 2001).

FAA faces challenges, including the need to enhance communication and teamwork, and to provide employees with the training and skills they need to operate effectively. For example, we have reported on FAA's implementation of management reforms, including delegating authorities to teams, to improve its rulemaking processes.[5] In our July 2001 report on aviation rulemaking we recommended, among other things, that the FAA Administrator take steps to (1) empower team members by giving them the authority to coordinate with the associate administrators (which would eliminate a separate review and approval step), (2) empower team members by permitting them to set their own schedules and deadlines, and (3) hold staff and management accountable for ensuring that schedules are realistic.

At IRS we identified the challenges the organization faces in revamping its human capital policies to help achieve its congressionally mandated transformation to an agency that better balances service to the taxpayers with enforcement of the tax laws.[6] IRS has made major changes to modernize its organization and operations and comply with the IRS Restructuring and Reform Act of 1998.[7] These changes present major management challenges and will require considerable time to successfully implement them, and IRS managers and employees are still learning how to work effectively in the new environment. In revamping its performance

[5] *Aviation Rulemaking: Further Reform Is Needed to Address Long-Standing Problems* (GAO-01-821, July 9, 2001).

[6] *Human Capital: Taking Steps to Meet Current and Emerging Human Capital Challenges* (GAO-01-965T, July 17, 2001).

[7] P.L 105-206, July 22, 1998.

management system, for example, we reported that IRS' new system is weakest at the front line, where interactions with taxpayers occur.[8] However, IRS officials told us that IRS is conducting customer satisfaction surveys to enhance its knowledge about what IRS employees can do to better meet taxpayers' needs.

VBA faces challenges in processing veterans' benefit claims accurately and in a timely manner. In its fiscal year 2000 performance report, the Veterans Administration reported that performance declined with respect to its rating-related claims-processing timeliness and national accuracy rate. Among the reasons it cited for this decline was underestimating how long it would take to realize the impact of initiatives such as increased staffing and improved training.[9] We reported that many experienced claims-processing staff are expected to retire and that VBA's training and recruitment programs may not be adequate to ensure a sufficient workforce of competent claims processors.[10] VBA officials told us that, in response to the concern we raised that many of the training modules might not be available in time to train new employees, VBA has stepped up implementation of its plans to use a new Training and Performance Support System (TPSS).[11] This

---

[8] *Follow-up to the May 8, 2001, Hearing Regarding the IRS Restructuring Act's Goals and IRS Funding* (GAO-01-903R, June 29, 2001), and *IRS Modernization: Continued Improvement in Management Capability Needed to Support Long-Term Transformation* (GAO-01-700T, May 8, 2001).

[9] *Veterans Affairs: Status of Achieving Key Outcomes and Addressing Major Management Challenges* (GAO-01-752, June 15, 2001).

[10] *Major Management Challenges and Program Risks: Department of Veterans Affairs* (GAO-01-255, Jan. 2001).

[11] *Veterans' Benefits: Training for Claims Processors Needs Evaluation* (GAO-01-601, May 31, 2001).

system is intended to provide standardized training to new employees who will replace the wave of employees expected to retire during the next several years. According to VBA officials, they are currently using TPSS training modules to facilitate the training of some new employees, but the training modules needed for other newly hired employees will not be available until November 2001. In the interim, VBA is using a web-based "field guide" to train those employees. The field guide uses a variety of delivery mechanisms including satellite broadcasts, video teleconferencing and centralized and localized classroom instruction.

FEMA also faces special mission-related challenges, including providing timely responses to disaster aid requests, preventing or reducing harm and losses from future disasters through cost-effective mitigation efforts, and working effectively with other federal, state, and local programs. To address its strategic human capital management challenges, FEMA has started an initiative to reduce middle management layers and streamline its organization.[12]

The fifth agency we report on—OPM—downsized significantly during the 1990s. Among its many responsibilities, OPM receives tens of thousands of federal employee claims for retirement and insurance benefits each year. Although its processes have not changed significantly since the 1980s, OPM plans to modernize its retirement systems. This modernization is OPM's central strategy to meet the long-term customer service and financial management objectives for CSRS and FERS. In its

[12] *Federal Emergency Management Agency: Status of Achieving Key Outcomes and Addressing Major Management Challenges* (GAO-01-832, July 9, 2001).

fiscal year 2002 performance plan OPM reported that, beginning in fiscal year 2002, it will phase in a new business model for retirement claims processing.[13]

## Scope And Methodology

To meet our objectives, we asked officials at five agencies to identify initiatives they had that empowered or involved employees. From the inventories of the initiatives they developed in response to our request, we asked agency officials to identify those agency components and initiatives that, in their view, had successfully involved and empowered employees. We sought to identify practices that were commonly implemented by the agencies within the past 5 years. In some cases, agencies focused our attention on practices that began earlier.

We interviewed agency executives, managers, supervisors, front-line employees, and union representatives to discuss how agencies had implemented these practices to empower and involve employees, and we analyzed related documents and information they provided. We did not attempt to verify the performance data that agencies provided.

We included FAA in our review because it has certain exemptions from the Federal Acquisition Regulations designed to facilitate delegating procurement authorities to lower levels. We included IRS and OPM in our review, given IRS' exemption from certain title 5 personnel provisions

[13] *Office of Personnel Management: Status of Achieving Key Outcomes and Addressing Major Management Challenges* (GAO-01-884, July 9, 2001).

and OPM's human capital leadership role in the federal government. FEMA and VBA were selected because a literature review of relevant articles indicated that front-line employees from those agencies had been empowered or involved in key agency decisions or operations.

Because we were seeking to review initiatives that had successfully empowered and involved employees, we asked headquarters officials to identify organizational components for our review. Our FAA work was concentrated at the Mike Monroney Aeronautical Center in Oklahoma City, OK. Our FEMA work was done at the National Security Affairs Office, the Response and Recovery Directorate, and the Operations Support Directorate within FEMA headquarters in Washington, D.C., and at FEMA's U.S. Fire Administration in Emmitsburg, MD. Our work at IRS was done at the Wage and Investment Division in IRS' headquarters in Washington, D.C., and at the Accounts Management, Submissions Processing, and Compliance branches at the Ogden, UT, Service Center. Our OPM work was conducted at its Retirement and Insurance Service locations in Washington, D.C., and Boyers, PA. Our VBA work was conducted at VBA's regional offices in Los Angeles, CA; Muskogee, OK; and Phoenix, AZ. Our selection process was not designed to provide examples that could be considered representative of all the employee empowerment and involvement initiatives at the agencies reviewed or the federal government in general.

We conducted our work from October 2000 through August 2001 in accordance with generally accepted government auditing standards.

## Six Key Practices Helped Empower And Involve Employees

The five agencies we reviewed implemented key empowerment and involvement practices as part of making organizational changes intended to realign organizations and processes to improve performance. The practices were (1) demonstrating top leadership commitment; (2) engaging employee unions in making changes; (3) training employees to enhance their knowledge, skills, and abilities; (4) using employee teams to help accomplish agency missions; (5) involving employees in planning, and sharing performance information; and (6) delegating authorities to front-line employees.

### Demonstrating Top Leadership Commitment

Top leadership commitment is crucial in developing a vision, initiating organizational change, maintaining open communications, and creating an environment that is receptive to innovation. In earlier reports and testimonies, we observed that top leadership must play a critical role in creating and sustaining high-performing organizations. Without the clear and demonstrated commitment of agency top leadership, organizational cultures will not be transformed, and new visions and ways of doing business will not take root.[14]

Consistent attention to employee empowerment and involvement issues helps to ensure that changes are sustained. Agency leaders need to commit their organizations to valuing and investing in their employees by empowering, involving, and providing them the tools to do their best, and by

---

[14] *Managing for Results: Federal Managers' Views Show Need for Ensuring Top Leadership Skills* (GAO-01-127, Oct. 20, 2000); *Management Reform: Using the Results Act and Quality Management to Improve Federal Performance* (GAO/T-GGD-99-151, July 29, 1999); and *Management Reform: Elements of Successful Improvement Initiatives* (GAO/TGGD-00-26, Oct. 15, 1999).

implementing the modern performance management and incentives systems needed to focus employees' efforts on achieving agency missions and goals. Top leadership commitment entails time, energy, and persistence in providing incentives and establishing accountability. Agency leaders must commit their organizations to valuing and investing in their employees and focusing their employees' efforts on achieving stated agency missions and goals.[15] While top leadership commitment can be demonstrated in many ways, the following are examples employees and managers identified for the selected initiatives we reviewed at these agencies.

- **Think strategically about areas where innovation would make good business sense.** Leaders conceptualized new approaches to improve performance and engaged employees and managers in shaping the implementation of that vision. For example, the Director at FAA's Logistics Center saw the need for operating more like a private sector business and envisioned the organizational and operational changes that would be required to do that. The Logistics Center's Director helped to ensure that all employees shared his vision by discussing proposed changes with his top-level managers and by meeting with front-line employees and union representatives to obtain their input about potential changes.
- **Reorganize and integrate operations.** Leaders implemented their visions by realigning their organizations to improve performance and increase the coordination of mission-related activities. For example, a Branch Chief in OPM's

[15] GAO-01-965T.

Retirement and Insurance Service enabled a new team to improve claims processing by, among other things, providing cross-training for the team to handle both CSRS and FERS claims.

- **Create an environment of trust and honest communication.** Leaders made themselves available to employees and unions, promoted open and constructive dialog, and were receptive to ideas and suggestions from employees at all levels. Following an approach to change management that is transparent and highly participatory is a key element in involving and empowering employees. For example, several of the agencies held town-hall meetings with employees to discuss workplace issues and provide a forum for input and feedback. IRS employees said that they felt that management used the information they provided about proposed changes.
- **Target investments and provide incentives to facilitate change.** Leaders provided funding and created financial and other incentives to support new ways of working and to encourage employees to attain the agencies' goals and objectives. For example, the FAA Logistics Center Director committed to providing every Logistics Center employee with a $500 cash award if the Center met all of its performance targets for fiscal year 2001. At the time of our review, the Logistics Center was on track to meet or exceed its goals.
- **Participate in efforts to benchmark successful organizations.** Some leaders visited organizations that were models for enhancing organizational flexibility and maintaining quality standards. By visiting and benchmarking model performance practices, leaders demonstrated to employees their personal commitment to making

the changes needed for their offices or units to become high-performing organizations.[16] For example, the Director of one VBA regional office visited several private sector organizations to observe how they processed claims and ensured accuracy. The insights gained were factored into the changes made in regional office claims operations.

- **Use a 360-degree performance feedback system.** One leader used input from team members to improve the team's performance. An OPM Branch Chief who supervises the cross-trained claims processing team implemented a 360-degree feedback system for assessing both her and her team members' performance. Under that system, team members provide her with input on her performance as a team coach as well as input on the performance of other team members. She then uses that information for self-assessment and in providing performance feedback to individual team members.

## Engaging Employee Unions

Involving employee unions, as well as involving employees directly, is crucial to achieving success. Major changes can involve redesigning work processes, changing work rules, developing new job descriptions, establishing new work hours, or making other changes to the work environment that are of particular concern to employees' unions. Obtaining union cooperation and support through effective labormanagement relations can help

[16] Benchmarking is a critical part of an effective improvement program because it helps an organization identify outstanding levels of performance that have actually been achieved. Benchmarking therefore helps define specific reference points for setting goals for improving performance. See *Managing for Results: Critical Actions for Measuring Performance* (GAO/T-GGD/AIMD-95-187, June 20, 1995).

achieve consensus on the planned changes, avoid misunderstandings, and more expeditiously resolve problems that occur. The following are examples of how agencies engaged employee unions.

- **Develop and maintain an ongoing working relationship with unions.** Agencies worked cooperatively with employee unions and found that an ongoing relationship enhanced communication. For example, OPM maintained a continuous dialog through weekly meetings of management and union representatives to share information and address workplace issues. Officials at OPM's Retirement Operations Center at Boyers, PA, and the American Federation of Government Employees (AFGE) said that their excellent working relationship helped facilitate the adjustments made to incorporate new technology at the Center. They said when new technology reduced the Center's need for file clerks, union and management officials worked together to ensure that affected employees received advance notice about upcoming changes, training in new skills, and information about available job opportunities.
- **Document formal agreements.** Agencies had formal agreements to serve as a foundation setting forth the manner in which labor and management would work together. For example, the agreement between IRS and the National Treasury Employees Union (NTEU) was designed to ensure that employees are adequately represented and informed of proposed new policies and have input into the proposals. The agreement also provides for continuous improvement in IRS operations in part by providing employees the authority, resources, and other inputs they need to effect changes and to be accountable for performing

effectively, and provides for NTEU participation in various forums, such as business process improvement teams and cross-unit committees.

- **Build trust over time.** Some agencies have undertaken a long-term effort to create an environment of trust and openness in working cooperatively with unions. For example, both IRS and NTEU officials credited the excellent working relationship they developed over the last decade for helping to reorganize IRS. Officials at IRS stated that the reorganization has resulted in operating divisions that are focused on serving taxpayers and flatter decision-making structures with clear end-to-end accountability. The NTEU President said that the union was willing to expedite some negotiations on mission-critical issues because a trusting relationship had developed and IRS employees felt that management used the information they provided in shaping the new IRS.
- **Participate jointly in making decisions.** Agencies involved unions and incorporated their input into proposals before finalizing decisions. For example, several unions provided suggestions about how agencies should share performance information with employees. In another instance, OPM's Operations Center and AFGE worked jointly on pre-decisional matters, such as the hiring of a new director of the Operations Center.

## Training Employees to Enhance Their Knowledge, Skills, and Abilities

Both employees and managers viewed training as a critical factor in learning how to work in new and different ways. To improve customer service, employees may need new skills, such as the ability to analyze and improve work processes or the ability to work effectively together on teams. In addition to job-specific skills and work processes, training in teamwork and communications and encouragement and coaching through mentoring and networking can help employees adapt to new ways of working that involve changes in their roles and job expectations. VBA officials, for instance, told us that, along with providing various training modules, employees also need on-the-job training, coaching and mentoring to enhance their expertise through actual experience in processing claims. The following are examples of how agencies trained employees in new processes.

- **Provide a mix of on-the-job and formal training.** Agencies used a variety of training techniques to help employees adjust to organizational and operational changes. For example, OPM provided on-the-job cross training so that a claims processing team could adjudicate both CSRS and FERS claims. According to the Branch Chief, because the team received cross-training, it was able to help another division reduce its backlog of FERS cases. OPM also provided formal training to teams in how to make decisions in setting goals, planning and assigning work, and scheduling overtime and training.
- **Provide training on building team relationships and new ways of working.** When making significant changes to their operations, agencies provided training to help facilitate change. For example, when IRS undertook a major reorganization, its Ogden, UT, Service Center trained its employees in the new ways of conducting business. The training workshops included (1) learning how effective teams function; (2) improving working

relationships among peers, managers and employees, and managers and union stewards; (3) enhancing effective communications among employees, union stewards, and managers; (4) increasing discussions about ways to improve work processes and meet customers' needs; and (5) creating a more positive workplace environment. The employees we interviewed said that training on effective working relationships was especially beneficial because they got to know their co-workers and gained an appreciation for each others' views.

- **Commit sufficient funding and time to training.** Agencies considered training needs in budget decisions and their workforce planning. For example, as FAA's Logistics Center was being reorganized to operate in a more businesslike manner, it trained employees about the need for, as well as on how to develop, quality work processes. This enabled employees to document information that was required for the Logistics Center to receive International Organization for Standardization (ISO) 9000 certification for quality work processes.[17] To receive this certification, an organization must show that it has standardized, high-quality processes that result in products and services that are provided in a timely manner.

[17] ISO is a worldwide federation of national standards bodies representing 140 countries. ISO 9000 certification recognizes standardized quality processes established by organizations to produce consistently high-quality products or services.

## Using Employee Teams To Help Accomplish Agency Missions

Adopting a teams-based approach to operations can improve employee morale and job satisfaction by creating an environment characterized by open communication, enhanced flexibility in meeting job demands, and a sense of shared responsibility for accomplishing agency goals and objectives. Using teams can also assist in integrating different perspectives, flattening organizational structure, and streamlining operations. In a prior GAO report on best practices, we said that commercial firms began using integrated product teams in the 1980s as a way to get better results faster.[18] An integrated product team is a concentration of product expertise within a team of employees who, together, have the authority to design, develop, test, manufacture, and deliver a product. In examining FAA's efforts to modernize its air traffic control systems, we stated that although FAA has identified an integrated team approach as key to the agency's efforts to deploy systems that meet performance goals, major offices still tended to function in stovepipes that inhibit an integrated team approach.[19]

The following are examples of how teams were used in the agency initiatives we reviewed.

- **Create teams of employees who represent multiple organizational functions and different grade levels.** Agencies flattened their organizational structures by including employees from various organizational functions and grade

[18] *Best Practices: DOD Teaming Practices Not Achieving Potential Results* (GAO-01-510, Apr. 10, 2001).

[19] *Air Traffic Control: Role of FAA's Modernization Program in Reducing Delays and Congestion* (GAO-01-725T, May 10, 2001).

levels on teams. For example, VBA consolidated regional office operations by merging two divisions and creating teams with members from both functions who could process claims from beginning to end. In some cases, forming teams provided opportunities for front-line employees to assume leadership roles. FEMA's teams at the U.S. Fire Administration provided opportunities for front-line employees to lead teams whose members included a mix of employees and supervisors. Agencies also took steps to streamline their processes by using a team approach. For example, VBA streamlined its claims process by allowing one employee to handle all aspects of a claim, instead of requiring employees to write referrals and wait for responses from other divisions. VBA's team approach also enhanced accountability to veterans because team members were responsible for handling specific claims.

- **Establish an integrated working environment with common goals.** When agencies established teams, this provided an environment in which individual team members were encouraged to work together toward achieving team goals. For example, FEMA's U.S. Fire Administration teams had members from units throughout the organization. The teams met on a weekly basis and identified ways to implement over 170 Board of Visitors recommendations for improving the Fire Administration's operations. These teams facilitated communications and employee involvement by maintaining a focal point for the organization, working toward consensus, and posting performance data showing progress toward addressing these recommendations.

- **Assign team responsibilities and provide an environment for learning.** Agencies assigned a broad range of responsibilities to teams and allowed members to help each other and learn new skills. For example, VBA's claims-processing teams were responsible for controlling claims from when first received until finally adjudicated. That required the team to conduct a full range of claims functions, including receiving and controlling the claims, contacting veterans and hospitals to obtain information, and making benefit decisions. Team members were able to assist other team members when needed, which helped develop team members' skills in functions they did not previously perform. To enable the team to efficiently meet their objectives, the teams were also responsible for setting their work schedules and managing their workload.
- **Hold teams accountable for results.** The agencies held teams accountable for accomplishing their work, and working together in a team environment encouraged team members to share accountability. When teams made decisions about how to do their work, employees told us they felt greater accountability for the teams' overall performance. For example, members of the FAA Logistics Center's integrated product teams were accountable for all aspects of the Center's products, including maintenance, repair, storage, and shipping. The teams' performance was measured on a regular basis, providing direct feedback to the teams.
- **Physically collocate team members when appropriate.** Agencies collocated team members when the employees had been working in the same building or facility. Although technology is being used to help

bring teams that are geographically dispersed together in a virtual environment, to the extent that team members are already located nearby, moving team members to a shared location improved communication and enhanced efficiency.[20] For example, collocating OPM's retirement team members facilitated the sharing of information among members and led to improved work processes and customer satisfaction.

## Involving Employees in Planning and Sharing Performance Information

Involving employees in planning and sharing performance information can help employees understand what the organization is trying to accomplish and how it is progressing in that direction. Involving employees in the planning process helps to develop agency goals and objectives that incorporate insights about operations from a front-line perspective, as well as increases employees' understanding and acceptance of organizational goals and objectives. Involving front-line employees in the goal-setting process also helps create a clear "line of sight" throughout the organization so that everyone understands what the organization is trying to achieve and the goals it seeks to reach. Employees we met with appeared committed to working toward the goals of their agencies and to providing high quality service.

Sharing performance information can provide employees with a more meaningful perspective

[20] Advances in the use of information technology and the Internet are continuing to change the way federal agencies communicate, use, and disseminate information, deliver services, and conduct business. See *Electronic Government: Challenges Must Be Addressed With Effective Leadership and Management* (GAO-01-959T, July 11, 2001).

about how their day-to-day activities contribute toward the organization's goals and objectives. Sharing performance information also allows supervisors to provide clearer and more specific feedback to teams and front-line employees on their expectations, progress, and performance. Agencies' use of performance information can be improved. In May 2001, we reported that, based on a survey of federal managers at 28 agencies, at no more than 7 of the 28 agencies surveyed did 50 percent or more of the managers respond that they used performance information to a great or very great extent.[21] However, at the agencies we visited, managers used performance information and shared this information with front-line employees through various mechanisms. Some of these agencies, such as VBA and IRS, used a balanced scorecard approach, which is intended to provide a balanced perspective regarding agency results, customer satisfaction, and employee feedback. At one of VBA's regional offices, for example, computerized information is continuously displayed on video screens providing employees with current performance information.

The employees we met with were aware of their agencies' and their units' performance goals and objectives, and they said that sharing performance information had enhanced communications across all levels of the organization. Employees told us that sharing performance information provided everyone with a focus to work toward and a status report on their progress. They also said that sharing performance information generated more performance-related discussions, including at

[21] *Managing for Results: Federal Managers' Views on Key Management Issues Vary Widely Across Agencies* (GAO-01-592, May 25, 2001).

town-hall meetings, other meetings with managers, and during team meetings.

The following are examples of how agencies involved employees in planning and sharing performance information.

- **Create mechanisms to involve employees in the planning process.** Agencies used various mechanisms to develop strategic plans, gather feedback from internal stakeholders for identifying gaps in existing strategic plans, and obtain employee input and feedback. For example, one IRS division used an employee team to help to develop its strategic plan. The team ensured that all division employees had opportunities to provide input, and the agency used that input as part of its efforts to develop a balanced set of goals and objectives for the division.
- **Post performance information throughout the workplace.** Agencies shared performance information with employees by posting it through a variety of means, including charts, graphs, newsletters, and agency intranet postings. For example, FAA's Logistics Center posted performance charts and graphs in the entry foyers of its buildings and at the entrances to its organizational units. Such postings permitted employees to easily see how their units' performance was contributing to agency goals and objectives. The Logistics Center also had a monthly newsletter for sharing organizational performance information and providing an arena for employees to share information.

- **Share performance information in meetings.** Agencies frequently held town-hall and other meetings to discuss program performance and organizational issues. Agencies used town-hall meetings to help employees better understand how their work efforts contributed to overall organizational success. The town-hall meetings also provided a forum in which employees and managers could discuss organizational changes and suggest operational improvements. For example, IRS' Ogden, UT, Service Center employees we interviewed said that for the first time regular and effective communications between Center managers and employees was occurring. They said that, in addition to listening, managers were taking action on employees' suggestions, which made the employees see that their input was valued. Frequent team meetings provided employees an opportunity to obtain feedback about agency performance. For example, VBA teams shared performance information at weekly meetings, information that helped the teams assess their progress in meeting performance goals.
- **Survey employees on their views regarding organizational direction.** Agencies used surveys to obtain employees' views, such as input regarding the direction of organizational changes. IRS' Wage and Investment Operating Division surveyed employees on the strengths, opportunities, and priorities for each of the division's branches, shared survey results with employees, and implemented changes as a result.

## Delegating Authorities to Front-line Employees

Delegating authorities to front-line employees involves the transfer of authorities from managers to those employees who are closer to citizens and provide services and information as part of their day-to-day activities. Providing delegated authorities can enable employees to control their own work processes and schedules. Delegating authorities also gives employees the opportunity to look at customer needs in an integrated way and effectively respond to those needs. Delegating authorities can benefit agency operations by streamlining processes. Furthermore, delegating authorities to front-line employees gives managers greater opportunities to concentrate on problems or policy-level issues. If employees believe they have the authority to tackle goals and objectives beyond their formal job descriptions and assigned units, then when customers have legitimate complaints, empowered front-line employees can "make it right" immediately rather than having to wait for management to get involved.

The following are examples of how agencies delegated authorities to front-line employees.

- **Empower on-site staff with authority to make decisions.** Agencies delegated authorities and empowered front-line employees to exercise responsibilities to more fully address customer needs. For example, FEMA public assistance coordinators are on-site at the disaster or emergency to observe the conditions and to coordinate public assistance. They were delegated the authority to determine applicants' eligibility, to approve up to $100,000 in public financial assistance, and to help to ensure that applicants are kept fully informed throughout the public assistance process.

- **Eliminate layers of review.** Agencies reduced the number of approvals needed for various activities and delegated greater authority to front-line employees to make decisions. For example, FAA's Aeronautical Center delegated authorities to its audiovisual teams to make decisions while on location, such as the need to visit locations in addition to those originally planned and approved. This allowed the audiovisual teams to more efficiently meet customer needs. At FEMA, delegating authority to the Public Assistance Coordinators eliminated two additional state reviews of applications for assistance and two other reviews by FEMA.
- **Provide more time for managers to focus on problem areas or policy matters**. Agencies targeted managers' skills on more difficult problems or policy areas by delegating some authorities to front-line employees. For example, VBA managers said they were able to use their time more efficiently after delegating day-to-day claims-processing authorities to the teams. They said that by delegating these authorities, they could concentrate on policy matters and more difficult problems that the teams were unable to handle.
- **Establish a new position with appropriate authority.** Some agencies identified situations in which new positions of authority could help benefit operations. For example, VBA, as part of its efforts to reengineer its claims processing, established a new decision review officer position and provided employees in those positions the authority to review and change claims decisions that veterans appealed. Prior to this, veterans' appeals were addressed under a formal hearing process. Because decision review officers have more flexibility to address appeals

informally, creating this new position provided the opportunity to streamline the process and save time.

## Agencies Addressed Barriers to Efforts That Empowered and Involved Employees

The agencies we reviewed undertook changes that represented a significant shift from their traditional operations and, as such, encountered organizational and cultural barriers that needed to be overcome as they sought to empower and involve employees. Some of the barriers included a lack of trust, resistance to change and a lack of buy-in, and implementation issues. Despite encountering these barriers, the employees and managers we met at each of the five agencies perceived benefits from the employee empowerment and involvement practices that their agencies had implemented. To address the barriers, the agencies used such strategies as open communication, a commitment to change, and providing performance feedback.

All of these efforts entailed cultural transformations, and therefore there was some natural resistance that took time and effort to overcome. Nevertheless, the experiences of these agencies demonstrate that organizations can make progress in addressing barriers to empower and involve their employees. The following are some examples of the barriers encountered and the strategies used to address them.

### Lack of Trust

The agencies identified a lack of trust as a barrier they experienced in their efforts to empower and involve employees. A lack of trust can frustrate agency attempts to implement major changes in employees' day-to-day working environment. Throughout our review, managers, unions, and employees continuously emphasized the importance of trust in gaining acceptance for changes. For example, some employees feared for their job security as FAA's Logistics Center began to implement more business like operations. However, they told us that they learned to trust the Logistics Center's Director as they recognized the need for the changes.

Some employees were skeptical that managers would listen to their input for planning purposes. They were also concerned that performance data would be used to justify punitive actions, rather than to increase employees' understanding about the direction of the agency's performance. In addition, working in a more open environment requires employees to trust and help each other, which some employees said initially was a barrier to working as a team. Maintaining an open door policy that encouraged employees to share their views and demonstrating a vision and commitment to change were two approaches that agencies used to develop trust.

## Resistance to Change and Lack of Buy-in

Another barrier that agencies experienced was resistance to change and a lack of buy-in. Employees and managers resisted making changes because they had to work in new and unfamiliar ways. Some employees found it difficult to transition from working under direct supervision to working on a team with little direct supervision. For example, according to FEMA officials, some team members continued to seek leadership and guidance from management, did not trust other team members, and were reluctant to speak out in the team environment until they eventually adjusted to working in a team environment.

According to officials from the five agencies, some managers found it difficult to operate in a new environment of more open communication and feedback. Some FEMA managers and supervisors were reluctant to allow employees to have delegated authorities in areas such as budgeting, procurement, and time and attendance report approval. At FAA's Aeronautical Center, some employees with contracting responsibilities were initially uncomfortable exercising newly delegated procurement authority to purchase goods or services up to a certain dollar amount without supervisory approval. The employees said that they gained confidence as they became more experienced in exercising the new authority, and some of the employees and managers who initially resisted changes adjusted to them gradually over time. In some cases, the offices we visited made managerial and supervisory changes when individuals were unable to adjust to a more open work environment.

A lack of buy-in resulted in some employees and managers being reluctant to fully participate in training. They tended to view the changes being made as another "flavor-of-the-month" initiative. Thus, they were not as open to receiving new information or adopting new ways of working. IRS provided an example of a solution to this barrier. To encourage managers to buy into team concept training, IRS has decided to train section chiefs who will then train employees in their work units.

## Implementation Issues

Implementation issues, such as workload demands and performance incentive issues, also presented barriers to change. Although employees generally appreciated the changes made to work in a team environment, high workload demands affected some team members' ability to exercise their delegated authority. VBA, for example, has a large, and growing, backlog of compensation and pension claims.[22] Although team members had the authority to set their schedules and determine their day-to-day work priorities, heavy workload demands prevented them from being able to plan and manage their work. Some of VBA's decision review officers also told us that their ability to exercise their delegated authorities had been limited by the claims-processing backlogs.

Another implementation issue that affected teams involved the incentives that agencies provided to teams to encourage performance. For example, some employees said that working on teams was demotivating when poor performers obtained an equal share of team rewards. Some employees and managers said that not enough money was available for rewarding employees and teams that met their goals and objectives. Such issues were commonly addressed in team meetings and in individual performance feedback.

The timing of training was another implementation issue that agencies cited as a barrier. For example, some team members told us that it would have been helpful if they had received training before being reorganized into teams, rather than after. Because training was not provided prior to moving to a team environment, the teams were immediately faced with the need for team members to take time off of the front lines for training and skill building. Providing training at the appropriate time for an employee can achieve better results.

[22] The accurate and timely processing of compensation and pension claims is one of the major management challenges we have identified at the Department of Veterans Affairs. See *Major Management Challenges and Program Risks: Department of Veterans Affairs* (GAO-01-255, Jan. 2001).

## Agencies Cited Examples of Performance Improvements

Agencies identified a range of examples to demonstrate the different ways performance can be improved in implementing the practices to empower and involve employees. As we have reported before when looking at management reform efforts, it is difficult to disentangle the effects of numerous initiatives and external factors that affect each agency's environment.[23] For example, external factors such as legislative changes that resulted in reopening nearly 100,000 veterans' claims and the increasing complexity of these claims have affected VBA's results in addressing its claims backlog.

Officials from the five agencies attributed improved operations to the employee empowerment and involvement initiatives they had implemented, and the specific offices we visited had achieved successes in implementing the practices we reviewed in this report. Therefore, these examples are presented to illustrate how performance can improve through the contributions of empowered and involved employees.

- FAA's Logistics Center Radar Product Division team addressed emergencies, as well as routine tasks, more quickly. Established in 1998, this Division is an integrated product team of experts such as engineers and electronic technicians, who perform all of the functions required to repair ground-based radar systems. In April 2000, the airport surveillance radar at Boston's Logan Airport was ripped from its mounting pedestal during severe weather conditions, severely reducing the number of flights in and

---

[23] *NPR's Savings: Claimed Agency Savings Cannot All Be Attributed to NPR* (GAO/GGD-99-120, July 23, 1999).

out of Logan Airport. Working together, the team, along with other FAA and non-FAA organizations, made extensive repairs and restored radar service within 58 hours after the incident. In December 2000, a similar problem occurred at New York's JFK airport, and the team restored service within 56 hours.

According to Logistics Center officials, prior to working as an integrated product team, it required longer for FAA to coordinate a response to similar emergencies and fully restore service. FAA said that collocating all of the logistics functions including Engineers, Items Managers, Technicians, Equipment Specialists, etc, allowed the team to work together on priority areas. Collocation also eliminated communication barriers, such as the need to write memos or leave voice mail messages to request services and wait for responses. Forming the team also allowed FAA to reduce overlapping roles and responsibilities. Logistics Center officials said that the Radar Product Division team's coordinated operations saved time, including reducing the average number of days required to obtain research assistance from 45 days to 1 day.

- FEMA's customer surveys show improved satisfaction. According to FEMA, one of its goals was to transform the public assistance program into a customer-driven and performance-based program, thereby improving the quality and delivery of service to state and local applicants. Customer surveys conducted by FEMA after each disaster where public assistance was provided showed that customer satisfaction has improved. Fiscal year 2000 survey results showed that 85.6 percent of the respondents were satisfied with the assistance FEMA provided, an increase from the 81.4 percent customer satisfaction level FEMA achieved in fiscal year 1999. FEMA's fiscal year 2001 target is to increase its customer satisfaction results up to 87 percent. FEMA officials we met with said that delegating authority to the employees in Public Assistance Coordinator positions had contributed to this improvement.

- OPM's retirement claims processing team helped another Division in the Retirement and Insurance Service reduce a backlog of retirement claims. In February 2000, there was a backlog of about 12,000 FERS retirement claims, and OPM's management instituted a seven-point plan to address this problem. One of the components of the plan was to provide an existing group of CSRS benefits specialists with cross training in FERS claims adjudication. OPM said that the team's flexibility, attitude, and work ethic played a significant role in the success of this effort, which was OPM's first cross-training initiative. According to OPM, the team's contribution, along with reallocating staff, hiring, and improved automation, led to a 7,000 case reduction in the backlog by March 2001.[24]

- IRS' Substitute for Return Authority has expedited taxpayer compliance. In some cases, IRS employees are authorized to prepare

[24] As reported in its fiscal year 2000 performance report, CSRS claims processing time increased to 44 days from 32 days in fiscal year 1999, and FERS processing times increased to more than 6 months from 3 months in fiscal year 1999 (see GAO-01-884). OPM has recognized the need to address lagging times in retirement claims processing. According to OPM, steps to implement its modernization plan have reduced FERS processing times, and development of a staffing plan will enable it to reduce CSRS processing times.

substitute tax returns for taxpayers that did not file or filed a false return. Instead of referring requests to a different office as was done in the past, IRS has delegated this authority to revenue officers. This allows one-stop case resolution, because the revenue officers now maintain complete control of the case through collection of any balance due. By streamlining IRS' processes, additional taxes are being assessed within 5 to 8 months, much faster than the 30 months it usually took before. This also benefits taxpayers, because the amount of penalties and interest added to taxpayer accounts is reduced when assessments are more timely. IRS reported that during a fiscal year 2000 pilot program, revenue officers with delegated authorities prepared 257 non-filer cases involving tax assessments of about $3.5 million.

- When VBA established its decision review officer position, it first used a pilot program to test the new operational approach at 12 locations. VBA found that during the pilot phase, which ended December 31, 2000, the number of appeals resolved at the regional office level increased by 10 percent. By implementing this position nationwide, VBA projects there will be a 45 percent increase in the number of appeals resolved at the regional offices during fiscal year 2001. VBA attributes the increased number of appeals resolved at the regional office level to the efforts of its decision review officers.

## Conclusions

As agencies plan and implement the President's initiative to restructure their workforces and streamline their organizations, they need to recognize how human capital contributes to achieving missions and goals. Effective changes can only be made and sustained through the cooperation of leaders, union representatives, and employees throughout the organization. All members of an organization must understand the rationale for making organizational and cultural changes because everyone has a stake in helping to shape and implement initiatives as part of agencies' efforts to meet current and future challenges. Agencies can improve their performance by the way they treat and manage their people.

In this report we have identified six key practices used in selected initiatives to help to empower and involve employees in identifying and implementing needed changes. These practices are

- providing sustained leadership commitment to open communications and support culture change,
- engaging unions to include all perspectives in achieving consensus about needed changes,
- using a variety of formal and on-the-job training approaches to facilitate the development of new skills,
- encouraging employees to combine their resources and talents by working together in teams,
- involving employees in planning and sharing performance information so that employees help shape agencies' goals and better understand how their day-to-day activities contribute to results, and
- empowering staff by giving them the authority they need to make decisions and effectively conduct agency operations.

Each federal agency will need to consider the applicability of these practices within the context of its own mission, needs, and culture. Nevertheless, we believe that agencies can improve their performance, enhance employees' morale and job satisfaction, and provide a working environment where employees have a better understanding of the goals and objectives of their organizations and how they are contributing to the results that American citizens want. We believe that the practices we identified should be considered by other agencies as they seek to improve their unique operations and respond to the challenges they are facing.

## Agency Comments

We provided drafts of this report in August 2001 to the Secretary of Veterans Affairs, the Secretary of Transportation, the Commissioner of Internal Revenue, the Director of the Office of Personnel Management, and the Administrator of the Federal Emergency Management Agency, or their designees, for their review. Cognizant agency officials from DOT, IRS, OPM, and FAA responded orally and agreed with the contents of the draft report. In some cases, they also provided written technical comments to clarify specific points regarding the information presented. Where appropriate, we have made changes to this report that reflect these technical comments. FEMA did not provide comments on this report.

As agreed with your office, unless you announce the contents of this report earlier, we plan no further distribution until 30 days after its issue date. At that time, we will send copies of the report to the Chairman, Subcommittee on Oversight of Government Management, Restructuring, and the District of Columbia, Senate Committee on Governmental Affairs; the Chairman and Ranking Member, Senate Committee on Governmental Affairs; and the Chairman and Ranking Member,

Subcommittee on Security, Proliferation, and Federal Services, Senate Committee on Governmental Affairs. We will also send copies to the Secretary of Veterans Affairs, the Secretary of Transportation, the Commissioner of Internal Revenue, the Director of the Office of Personnel Management, and the Administrator of FEMA. In addition, we will make copies available to others upon request.

If you have any questions about this report, please contact me or Susan Ragland on (202) 512-6806. Others who contributed to this report were N. Scott Einhorn, Shirley Bates, Tom Beall, Gerard Burke, Renee Chafitz, Sharon Hogan, Cassandra Joseph, John Lesser, Michelle Sager, and Greg Whitney.

Sincerely yours,

J. Christopher Mihm
Director, Strategic Issues

# Related GAO Products


*Managing For Results: Federal Managers' Views Show Need for Ensuring Top Leadership Skills* (GAO-01-127, Oct. 20, 2001).

*Veterans Affairs: Status in Achieving Key Outcomes and in Addressing Major Management Challenges* (GAO-01-752, June 15, 2001).

*Veterans Benefits: Training for Claims Processors Needs Evaluation* (GAO-01-601, May 31, 2001).

*Managing For Results: Federal Managers' Views on Key Management Issues Vary Widely Across Agencies* (GAO-01-592, May 25, 2001).

*Best Practices: DOD Teaming Practices Not Achieving Potential Results* (GAO-01-510, Apr. 10, 2001).

*High-Risk Series: An Update* (GAO-01-263, Jan. 2001).

*Major Management Challenges and Program Risks: Department of Transportation* (GAO-01-253, Jan. 2001).

*Major Management Challenges and Program Risks: Department of the Treasury* (GAO-01-254, Jan. 2001).

*Major Management Challenges and Program Risks: Department of Veteran Affairs* (GAO-01-255, Jan. 2001).

*Major Management Challenges and Program Risks: Department of Veterans Affairs* (GAO-01-255, Jan. 2001).

*Veterans Benefits Administration: Problems and Challenges Facing Disability Claims Processing* (GAO/T-HEHS/AIMD-00-146, May 18, 2000).

*Veterans Benefits: Promising Claims-Processing Practices Need to be Evaluated* (GAO/HEHS-00-65, Apr. 7, 2000).

*Veterans Benefits Administration: Progress Encouraging, but Challenges Still Remain* (GAO/T-HEHS-99-77, Mar. 25, 1999).

# Index

Page numbers followed by "f" denote figures

A
ABC Foundation case study
  discussion, 148–150
  introduction, 139–142
  Knowledge Initiative Advisory Committee, 147
  knowledge management
    initiatives, 145–148
    success factors, 142–145, 148–149
  knowledge sharing
    description of, 151–152
    effectiveness inventory, 155–165
    proficiencies in, 152–155
Abramson, Mark, 25
Aerospace industry, 24–25, 25f
Agency for International Development, 17
AIAA. *see* American Institute for Aeronautics and Astronautics
Allee, Verna, 85
American Institute for Aeronautics and Astronautics, 22
American Society for Training and Development, 35
Amidon, Debra, 140
Audit, knowledge, 68–69
Avery, Napoleon, 40

B
Barr, Stephen, 135–136
Beazley, Hamilton, 78
Beck, Nuala, 131
Behavioral change, 109
Benchmarking, 43, 185–186
Benne, Kenneth, 109
Bennis, Warren, 109
Berens, Michael, 53
Bernacki, Ed, 45
"Best practiced" organizations, 8
Bigornia, Boni, 33
Bontis, Nick, 52–53
Brower, Dana, 122
Bruzzese, Anita, 78
Bureau of Labor Statistics, 4, 16, 46–47
Bush, George W., 31–32, 123, 136
Businesses. *see* Industry; Organization
Business management competencies, 94

C
Cabral, John, 111
Canada
  competency-based management in, 49, 102–103
  human capital shortage in, 4, 26
  knowledge sharing in, 104

Capital
human. *see* Human capital
intellectual
definition of, 2, 101–102
measuring of, 127, 131–132
university partnering to stimulate, 125–126
social, 121–122
structural, 2, 64, 121
Case study
discussion, 148–150
introduction, 139–142
Knowledge Initiative Advisory Committee, 147
knowledge management
initiatives, 145–148
success factors, 142–145, 148–149
knowledge sharing
description of, 151–152
effectiveness inventory, 155–165
proficiencies in, 152–155
Caterinicchia, Dan, 111
Change
behavioral, 109
champion of, 108
employee training for, 189
incentives to facilitate, 185
inevitability of, 105, 116
psychological adaptation to, 106
resistance to, 58, 105–106, 201–202
steps involved in, 107–108
Change management
description of, 48, 57
examples of, 106–107
in knowledge management strategy, 69, 107–111, 114–116
at Los Alamos Laboratory, 106–107
at NASA
description of, 58–59, 111–112
Integrated Financial Management Program, 112–114
practices for, 58
strategies for, 109–111
traditional approaches to, 108
trust and, 110
CHCO. *see* Chief Human Capital Officer
Chen, Ernie, 81
Chief Human Capital Officer
attributes of, 10–11
Chief Knowledge Officers and, 10
creation of, 9, 127–128
functions of, 5–6
Human Resources Director and, 5, 10–11
industry uses, 6
Chief Information Officers, 9
Chief Knowledge Officers
Chief Human Capital Officer and, 10
competencies of, 10, 53
description of, 9
importance of, 128
responsibilities of, 53
Summit for the Public Sector, 109
Chin, Robert, 109
CIO. *see* Chief Information Officers
Civilian workforce
at Department of Defense, 19
at NASA, 19, 21–22
reductions in, 19
CKOs. *see* Chief Knowledge Officers
Combination, 87
Communication, 55, 163, 185
Communications, 94
Competencies
business management, 94, 97
human resources, 97–98
knowledge sharing of, 103–104
professional, 94, 97
proficiency levels for, 94–95
strategic. *see* Strategic competencies
Competency management
description of, 48–50, 93

frameworks for
Canadian models, 102–103
Federal Highway Administration, 93–95
international examples of, 98–99
National Academy of Public Administration, 95
State Government of Maine, 98
human resources models
Department of Defense, 97–98
Office of Personnel Management, 95–96
model for, 95
performance management and, 93
Content management, 70–71
Creative leadership groups, 91
Cross, Rob, 128–129
Culture
knowledge management, 68–69
knowledge sharing, 103–104, 115, 128, 163
organization. *see* Organization culture
performance. *see* Performance culture
Cunningham, Ian, 35
Customer capital, 2, 64

D
Davenport, Tom, 128
Department of Defense
civilian workforce reductions, 19
hiring cutbacks, 18
human resources competency model, 97–98
Department of Energy, 18
Department of Interior, 120
Department of Veterans Affairs, 18
Dietrick, William, 67, 71

E
E-learning, 35
Employees
annual performance plan for, 82
as asset, 111, 127
bonding, 87
brainpower of, 1, 11, 151
collective talent of, 1
commitment to knowledge by, 52
competitive edge provided by, 127
costs of replacing, 4
decision making by, 198
delegation of authority, 175, 198–200
developmental opportunities for, 91
education of, 132
empowerment practices
barriers to, 200–203
delegation of authority, 198–200
employee involvement in planning and sharing of performance information, 194–197
employee teams used to accomplish agency missions, 191–194
employee unions, 186–188
implementation issues, 202–203
leadership commitment, 183–186
overview of, 175, 208
training, 188–190
importance of, 1
intrinsic motivation of, 141, 149
lack of buy-in by, 202
lack of trust by, 200–201
performance information shared with, 194–197
rewards for knowledge management, 69, 82–83
statistics regarding, 45–46
training of, 91, 115, 132, 175, 188–190, 203
transformation of, 61–62
turnover of, 24
voluntary departure by, 24
work span for, 4
Employee teams, 191–194
Employee unions
agreements with, 187–188

Employee unions (continued)
  description of, 175
  engaging of, 186–188
  joint decision making with, 188
  relationship with, 187
Externalization, 87
Extrinsic rewards, 83

F
FAA. *see* Federal Aviation Administration
Fairhall, Lisa, 62
Federal Aviation Administration, 101, 178, 204–205
Federal Emergency Management Agency, 180, 192, 205–206
Federal Executive Institute, 122
Federal government
  citizen-centered, 137
  GAO Human Capital Report, 169–210
  human capital crisis in
    cornerstones of, 36
    description of, 3
    hiring practices, 15–16
    information technology employees, 16
    outsourcing effects, 28
    reasons for, 17–19
    shifts in orientation of, 34
    statistics regarding, 15–16
    success factors for, 36–37
  learning strategies for, 35
  market-based, 137
  performance management, 51–52
  reform initiatives, 135–137
  results-oriented, 137
  university partnerships with, 123, 125
  workforce
    downsizing of, 18, 28
    information technology, 16
    reductions in, 17
    reforming of, 15–16
    retiring of, 15
Federal Highway Administration, 93
Federal Workforce Improvement Act of 2002, 26–28
Feedback, 186
FEMA. *see* Federal Emergency Management Agency
Ferdinand, Pamela, 16–17
FHWA. *see* Federal Highway Administration
Figura, Susannah, 6
Fitz-enz, Jack, 52, 130
Foreign governments, 25–26
Fryer, Shari, 129

G
GAO Human Capital Report, 169–210
Gardner, Nicole, 25
General Services Administration, 122–123
Gonzales, Angela, 23
Gottschalk, Petter, 110
Government. *see* Federal government
Government Performance and Results Act, 51

H
Hanley, Sue, 72
Health Physics Society, 3–4
Hiring
  cutbacks in, 18–19
  retirees, 115–116
  time reductions for, 15–16
Human capital
  business success and, 33
  definition of, 2, 121
  entities, 117
  factors that affect, 4
  framework for, 6–7, 40
  government crisis. *see* Federal government, human capital crisis in

growth of, 132–133
knowledge management linked to, 11–14, 34–35, 79
online communities effect on, 124–125
principles of, 7
reforms in, 136–137
shareholder value and, 32
shortage of, 3–4
sources of, 11
U.S. Government concerns, 3
Human Capital Assessment and Accountability framework, 40
Human capital management
competency management, 48–50
knowledge management. *see* Knowledge management
measurements of, 130–131
performance management, 48, 50–51
strategic. *see* Strategic human capital management
Human Capital Scorecard, 6–7, 37
Human capital strategy
approach for constructing, 42–44
change management in, 111
competency management in, 103–104
at Department of Interior, 120–121
essentials of, 48–59, 117–118
innovation benefits, 118
knowledge management in, 74–75
lack of, 119
managing of, 117–118
models, 31–32, 36
NASA Goddard Space Flight Center, 43–44
pillars of, 128. *see also specific pillar*
Human resources
preparations for aging workforce, 130
rating of, 6
Human resources competency models
Department of Defense, 97–98
Office of Personnel Management, 95–96
Human Resources Director
Chief Human Capital Officer and, 5, 10–11
description of, 5
Human Resources Management Council, 27, 31
Hurt, John, 123–124

I
Industry
aerospace, 24–25, 25f
chief human capital officer in, 6
competency-based management in, 49–50
competitive advantage in, 24
human capital shortage in
description of, 4
shareholder value effects, 32–33
statistics regarding, 23–24
knowledge sharing in, 151–152
Informal learning, 128
Information technology workforce
retiring of, 16
shortages in, 16
Innovation
description of, 35–36
elements to stimulate, 141
examples of, 144
human capital strategy and, 118
knowledge management and, 139–141
leadership commitment to, 184
organizational renewal through, 141
processes involved in, 140
Integrated Financial Management Program, 58–59, 112–114
Intellectual capital
definition of, 2, 101–102
measuring of, 127, 131–132
university partnering to stimulate, 125–126
Internalization, 87

Internal Revenue Service, 40–42, 178–179, 206–207
International Organization for Standardization 9000, 190
Intrinsic motivation, 141, 149
Intrinsic rewards, 82–83

J
Job applicants
  future for, 78
  recruiting of, 28
  training of, 28

K
Kelmen, Steven, 108–109
Khandelwal, Vijay, 110
Knowledge
  application of, 56
  as asset, 141
  capture of, 54
  communication of, 55
  community of, 140–141
  creation of, 57, 85–86
  employee commitment to, 52
  identification of, 54
  incorporation of, 56
  reuse of, 56, 164
  sources of, 11
  strategy for acquiring, 35–36
  taxonomy of, 149–150
  visceral, 141
Knowledge audit, 68–69, 83
Knowledge-centric organization, 142
Knowledge gaps, 83
Knowledge management
  ABC Foundation case study of
    initiatives, 145–148
    success factors, 142–145, 148–149
  adaptability/agility gained from, 64–65, 100
  benefits of, 78
  budgeting for, 66
  business uses of, 3, 66
  capital used in, 2, 63–64
  change management and, 69, 107–111, 114–116
  closed-loop system, 82
  collaborative environment for, 71
  community-based model, 140
  components of, 52, 64, 151
  core competencies and, 13
  corporate users of, 4–5
  cost savings of, 5
  creativity from, 65, 100
  crossfunctional team for, 66, 68
  definition of, 11, 63
  description of, 48, 52
  governance of, 67–68
  human capital linked to, 11–14, 34–35, 79
  importance of, 63
  initiatives, 72, 140, 143
  innovation and, 139–141
  institutional memory building from, 65, 100
  intellectual capital, 2
  leader of, 66
  leadership and, 143
  measures and measurement of, 72, 143–144
  metrics to evaluate, 143–144
  at NASA Goddard Space Flight Center, 12f, 12–13
  organizational facilitation for, 164
  organization use of, 12–13, 53, 65–66, 100–101
  ownership considerations, 68–69
  people-to-people connection benefits, 88
  performance management effects on, 80–91
  principles of, 34

processes involved in, 55–57, 64, 81
reasons for adopting, 3, 66
rewards used in, 69, 82–83
skeptics of, 13–14
software for, 134–135
steps involved in, 42, 52–53
strategic framework for
application, 71
components of, 67
content management, 70–71
culture, 68–69
description of, 13, 67, 84f, 84–85
enablers of, 85
governance, 67–68
implementation of, 73–75
measurement, 72
models, 87
technology, 71, 134–135
success factors, 64–66, 100–101, 142–145
surveys of, 66
sustainment of, 143
technology for, 71, 134–135
terminology for, 14
trends in, 135
value created by, 99–100
Knowledge map, 70, 83
Knowledge professionals, 81–82
Knowledge ratio, 131
Knowledge retention managers, 70–71
Knowledge sharing
ABC Foundation case study of
description of, 151–152
effectiveness inventory, 155–165
proficiencies in, 152–155
barriers to, 119–120
Canadian models of, 104
communication for, 163
competencies, 103–104
culture of, 103–104, 115, 128, 163
description of, 11, 52, 55, 69
effectiveness inventory, 155–165
industry examples of, 151–152
internalization secondary to, 75
at NASA, 119–120
proficiencies in, 152–155
socialization secondary to, 75
Knowledge spiral, 86f, 86–87
Knowledge stewards, 70
Kotter, John, 107

L
Labor force. *see* Workforce
Leadership
commitment by, 175, 183–186
definition of, 7
goals for, 38
knowledge management uses, 143
measures, 38
success factors, 40
Learning
environment for, 193
in federal agencies, 35
goals, 39
informal, 128
knowledge strategy and, 35–36, 85
measures for, 39
online communities for, 133
organizational, 133–134
from strategic partnerships, 124
strategies for, 35
success factors, 40
"Learning" organization, 11, 69, 75
Learning pillar, 7
Legislation
Federal Workforce Improvement Act of 2002, 26–28
types of, 48
Lewis, Bob, 107–108
Liebowitz, Jay, 83, 85
London Business School, 117–118
Los Alamos Laboratory, 106–107

M
Macdonald, Andy, 108
Management. *see* Change management; Competency management; Knowledge management; Performance management
McDermott, Richard, 88
Megbolugbe, Isaac, 85
Mentoring, 11, 75
META Group, 24
Mihm, Chris, 61
Mitchell, Michael, 53
Morella, Constance, 17, 28
Munoz, Michael, 63

N
NAPA. *see* National Academy of Public Administration
NASA
- change management at, 58–59, 111–112
- civilian workforce reductions, 19, 21–22
- cultural change at, 111
- employee development directives, 115
- Goddard Space Flight Center
  - human capital crisis at, 3, 17
  - human capital strategy at, 43–44
  - knowledge management at, 12f, 12–13, 75
  - knowledge preservation project at, 116
  - online community, 88, 89f
- hiring
  - cutbacks in, 18
  - statistics regarding, 21–22
- human capital crisis at
  - corrective actions for, 22–23, 119
  - description of, 3, 17
  - statistics regarding, 19, 21–22
  - strategies to change, 119
- Integrated Financial Management Program, 58–59, 112–114
- knowledge sharing at, 119–120
- Lessons Learned Information System, 74–75
- organizational development directives, 115
- Senior Executive Service workforce at, 19, 20f

National Academy of Public Administration, 95
National Science Foundation, 123–124
National Treasury Employees Union, 187–188
Neilson, Robert, 53
Networks
- community-based, 140
- informal, 128–129
- social, 83–84, 118, 124

Newell, Terry, 122
Nguyen, Bao, 115
Norton, David, 111
NRC. *see* Nuclear Regulatory Commission
NTEU. *see* National Treasury Employees Union
Nuclear Regulatory Commission, 17

O
Office of Management and Budget, 31
Office of Personnel Management
- description of, 27, 31, 37, 50, 80
- employee union relationships, 187
- human resources competency model, 95–96
- performance improvements at, 206
- workforce changes, 180–181

O'Keefe, Sean, 111
Older workers
- human resources response, 130
- statistics regarding, 129

OMB. *see* Office of Management and Budget

Online communities
  development of, 133
  human capital strengthened by, 124–125
  learning benefits of, 133
  nurturing of, 143
  organization use of, 87–88
  strategic partnerships enhanced by, 125
OPM. *see* Office of Personnel Management
Organization
  "best practiced," 8
  change in, 58
  core competencies of, 13
  effectiveness of, 65–66, 100–101
  human capital strategy for, 42–43
  informal networks in, 128–129
  innovation benefits for, 141
  intellectual capital for, 101–102
  knowledge-centric, 142
  knowledge management at, 12–13, 53, 65–66, 100–101
  "learning," 11, 69, 75
  learning in, 133–134
  mission of, 11
  model for, 8
  online communities used by, 88
  performance information shared with employees, 194–197
  policies of, 7
  realignment of, 184–185
  renewal of, 141
  resistance to change, 105–106
  transformation of, 8, 61–62
  trust in, 110
Organizational alignment, 7
Organizational intelligence, 133–134, 141
Organization culture
  changes in, 57, 63
  transformation of, 8, 61–62
Outsourcing, 28, 126

P
Parker, Marilyn, 57
Partnerships, strategic
  building of, 121–122
  at Department of Interior, 120–121
  importance of, 121, 127
  learning from, 124
  at NASA, 119–120
  National Science Foundation, 123–124
  online communities effect on, 125
  private-public, 122–123
  university-government, 123, 125
Patent-to-stock price ratio, 131
Pay-sharing system, 28–29
Peckenpaugh, Jason, 15
Pederson, Larry, 81
Performance culture
  definition of, 7
  goals, 39
  measures for, 39
  success factors, 40
Performance improvements
  examples of, 204–207
  incentives to promote, 203
  information sharing with employees, 194–197
Performance management
  benefits of, 77
  description of, 48, 50–51
  goal-setting framework for, 84
  in human capital strategy, 78
  international programs of, 78
  key points of, 77
  knowledge management and, 80–91
  planning of, 83
  processes involved in, 80
Private-public strategic partnerships, 122–123
Prusak, Larry, 128–129
Public Service of Canada, 102–103

R
Research-to-development ratio, 131
Retirees, 115–116
Return-on-knowledge assets, 131
Rezendes, Victor, 8–9
Ringer, Richard, 106–107
Roles
  defining of, 93
  example of, 93–94
Ronayne, Peter, 122

S
Sebra, Bill, 4
Seeley, Chuck, 67, 71
Senior Executive Service workforce, 19, 20f
Shareholder value, 32–33
Skyrme, David, 35–36
Social capital, 121–122
Socialization, 75, 87
Social networks, 83–84, 118, 124
Social Security Administration
  human capital crisis at, 17
  international partnerships, 122
  mentoring at, 33
Sohal, Amrik, 105
SSA. *see* Social Security Administration
State Government of Maine competency management framework, 98
Storytelling, 149
Strategic alignment and planning
  focus of, 7, 37
  measures for, 37
  performance goals for, 37
  success factors, 40
Strategic competencies
  definition of, 7, 38
  measures, 38
  performance goals, 38
  success factors, 40
Strategic human capital management
  approaches to, 9
  government department rating in, 32
  steps involved in, 62–63
Strategic partnerships
  building of, 121–122
  at Department of Interior, 120–121
  importance of, 121, 127
  learning from, 124
  at NASA, 119–120
  National Science Foundation, 123–124
  online communities effect on, 125
  private-public, 122–123
  university-government, 123, 125
Strategy for human capital. *see* Human capital strategy
Stress, 46
Strong, Kelly, 106–107
Structural capital, 2, 64, 121
Sydanmaanlakka, Pentti, 81

T
Talent
  definition of, 7, 38
  measures, 38
  performance goals, 38
  success factors, 40
Teams
  accountability of, 193
  integrated working environment for, 192
  relationships among, 189–190
Tenney, Judy, 22
Thompson, Fred, 51–52
360-degree performance feedback system, 186
Training of employees, 91, 115, 132, 175, 188–190, 203
Trust, 110, 185, 188, 200–201

U
Unions. *see* Employee unions
Universities
  knowledge sharing proficiencies, 153–154

partnerships
with government, 123, 125
intellectual capital stimulated through, 125–126
U.S. Forest Service, 18, 33

V
Veterans' Benefits Administration, 179–180, 207
Voinovich, George, 15, 26
Volcker, Paul, 136

W
Waddell, Dianne, 105
Walker, David, 16, 18, 33–34, 48, 79, 118–119
Weinstock, Matthew, 17
Wellner, Alison, 129
Wenger, Etienne, 135
Workforce
civilian
at Department of Defense, 19
at NASA, 19, 21–22
reductions in, 19
federal government
aging of, 78, 129–130
competencies for, 93
competitive edge, 115
downsizing of, 18, 28
information technology, 16
median ages, 47
reductions in, 17
reforming of, 15–16
retiring of, 15
roles for, 93
statistics regarding, 45–46
Working environment, 192

Z
Zimmerman, Eilene, 130